# Hurricane Katrina

## Lessons for Army Planning and Operations

Lynn E. Davis, Jill Rough, Gary Cecchine, Agnes Gereben Schaefer, Laurinda L. Zeman

Prepared for the United States Army
Approved for public release; distribution unlimited

RAND ARROYO CENTER

The research described in this report was sponsored by the United States Army under Contract No. W74V8H-06-C-0001.

**Library of Congress Cataloging-in-Publication Data**

Hurricane Katrina : lessons for army planning and operations / Lynn Davis ... [et al.].
    p. cm.
    Includes bibliographical references.
    ISBN 978-0-8330-4167-8 (pbk. : alk. paper)
    1. Military planning—United States. 2. Armed forces—Civic action—United
States. 3. Hurricane Katrina, 2005. 4. Disaster relief—Gulf States. I. Davis, Lynn.

U153.H87 2007
363.34'8—dc22

2007017599

The RAND Corporation is a nonprofit research organization providing objective analysis and effective solutions that address the challenges facing the public and private sectors around the world. RAND's publications do not necessarily reflect the opinions of its research clients and sponsors.

**RAND®** is a registered trademark.

Published 2007 by the RAND Corporation
1776 Main Street, P.O. Box 2138, Santa Monica, CA 90407-2138
1200 South Hayes Street, Arlington, VA 22202-5050
4570 Fifth Avenue, Suite 600, Pittsburgh, PA 15213-2665
RAND URL: http://www.rand.org/
To order RAND documents or to obtain additional information, contact
Distribution Services: Telephone: (310) 451-7002;
Fax: (310) 451-6915; Email: order@rand.org

# Preface

Hurricane Katrina was a truly catastrophic domestic emergency, both in the number of deaths and the untold damage and destruction caused by the storm. The Army asked the RAND Arroyo Center to assess the Army response to Hurricane Katrina and to raise the critical issues for future Army planning and operations. This book focuses on those problems that most affected the timeliness and robustness of the Army's response to Hurricane Katrina. It explores steps that the Army, in both its active-duty and National Guard components, can take to improve its responsiveness, within the constraints inevitable in situations involving such catastrophic destruction. This publication will be of interest to anyone concerned with how the nation should prepare to respond to future catastrophic events, not only to severe hurricanes and other natural disasters but also to potential terrorist attacks.

This research was sponsored by the Commander of U.S. Army Forces Command (FORSCOM). It was conducted within the RAND Arroyo Center's Strategy, Doctrine, and Resources Program. RAND Arroyo Center, part of the RAND Corporation, is a federally funded research and development center sponsored by the United States Army.

The Project Unique Identification Code (PUIC) for the project that produced this document is DAPRR06017.

For more information on RAND Arroyo Center, contact the Director of Operations (telephone 310-393-0411, extension 6419; FAX 310-451-6952; email Marcy_Agmon@rand.org), or visit Arroyo's web site at http://www.rand.org/ard/.

# Contents

# Figures

# Tables

# Summary

Hurricane Katrina was a catastrophic domestic emergency that, in its deaths and destruction, had many of the possible characteristics of future terrorist attacks, especially those that could occur simultaneously in different parts of the United States or involve the use of weapons of mass destruction. It thus provides a case study that will help further our understanding of the problems that can arise during the nation's response to such an event. Such a case study will also help to determine how the United States might better prepare to respond to future catastrophic domestic emergencies.

The efforts undertaken by civilian and military organizations in response to Hurricane Katrina were historically unprecedented. But, as the many "lessons-learned" reports generated to date have documented, the response was tragically inadequate. Having researched what happened, we focused our analysis on the problems that affected the outcome of the response to Hurricane Katrina in a major way. The single most important problem was the speed with which the nation's local, state, and federal civilian organizations were overwhelmed. However, problems also arose in the military response in the critical first few days of the response, problems that contributed to the delays in evacuating the Superdome and convention center in New Orleans and in accomplishing search and rescue operations throughout the storm-ravaged areas of Louisiana and Mississippi.

The lessons-learned reports focus on the time it took for both the National Guard and active land forces to arrive in the region. Examining the considerations that influenced the size and timing of these deployments, we found that the experience of Hurricane Katrina suggests that the characteristics of the National Guard response to that event may be close to the kind of response the nation can expect from the Guard in such future emergencies, given the reliance on volunteers among those guardsmen responding from outside the stricken states and on air (commercial and military) and ground transportation.

Many considerations lay behind the timing of President Bush's decision to deploy active-duty Army and Marine land forces. The primary reasons this decision was not reached sooner were the administration's belief that the flow of National Guard forces would be sufficient and its reluctance to have active-duty forces involved in the deteriorating law-enforcement environment. Even had the decision to deploy active-duty forces been made at the time of hurricane landfall, the time lines for readying and transporting these forces would still not have had them on the scene and engaged in response operations until after the evacuations of the New Orleans Superdome and New Orleans Convention Center had been completed.

Another problem in the military's response to Hurricane Katrina highlighted in the lessons-learned reports is the lack of a unified command and control ($C^2$) structure, specifically the separation of the command structures for operations involving both National Guard and active-duty forces. We examined the characteristics of the multiple and complex $C^2$ structures employed during the Hurricane Katrina response efforts and could not find a direct link with the speed and efficiency of the military response.

Once we developed an understanding of the events that occurred during the response to Hurricane Katrina, we turned to ways the Army's response to future catastrophic domestic emergencies could be made quicker and more robust. We identified a number of steps that could be taken to enhance a future National Guard response on the part of states and urge their adoption: Give the National Guard the federal mission to conduct homeland security (HLS) activities,[1] as is

---

[1]   By "HLS," we mean military activities in support of civilian organizations, i.e., those involved in preventing and responding to terrorist attacks as well as in responding to other kinds of domestic emergencies, including natural disasters and civil disturbances. These

the case today in counterdrug operations; make *each* National Guard unit capable of rapid deployment; plan on having units ready to fill in for those deployed overseas; prepare governors to call up their units involuntarily to state active duty for out-of-state emergencies; and plan to use the Air National Guard, or prepare plans to use commercial airlines, to transport predesignated National Guard units to out-of-state emergencies.

At a regional level, we see the need for steps that would dedicate National Guard units to HLS and have them work closely with the Federal Emergency Management Agency and other civilian organizations. The creation of ten standing homeland security task forces, as recommended in our earlier report *Army Forces for Homeland Security*, deserves support and is in line with the Army Campaign Plan's regional approach to meeting HLS requirements in the National Guard.[2]

The Army's Force Generation (ARFORGEN) process, whereby units move through a structured and predictable process of unit readiness over time, offers additional possibilities to improve the military's readiness to respond to a catastrophic event, and these possibilities deserve serious consideration. Some National Guard units could be given HLS as their mission, with their training and readiness tailored accordingly. To achieve a quick and robust response to catastrophic emergencies, National Guard and active-duty Army units in the Available pool could be designated for an HLS mission. While in the ARFORGEN process these units would be designated as "theater committed" and planned for use within the United States, they could still be deployed overseas if needed.

The issue of how to structure the military $C^2$ arrangements will always emerge in responses to domestic emergencies. Given the obstacles to deciding on a structure in advance of events and the drawbacks

---

activities encompass what the Department of Defense calls Defense Support to Civil Authorities (DSCA).

[2]  See U.S. Army, Army Campaign Plan, Annex F (ARFORGEN Implementation Plan) to Army Campaign Plan Change 4, July 27, 2006, p. F-4-C-7. For a more detailed description of characteristics of these homeland security task forces, including the training, personnel, legal issues, and command and control, see Lynn E. Davis et al., *Army Forces for Homeland Security*, Santa Monica, Calif.: RAND Corporation, MG-221-A, 2004, pp. 31–37.

of having the structure emerge slowly over time (as happened in the response to Hurricane Katrina), we urge the adoption of an approach that would prepare decisionmakers to quickly select from a set of pre-defined alternative $C^2$ structures designed to give the lead to federal or state task forces, depending on the characteristics of the emergency.

Some of these recommendations will cost money, but what is most needed is a change from past practices and in perspectives on the role and responsibility of the military in catastrophic domestic emergencies. Having military forces trained and ready for homeland security is no less important than for contingencies overseas.

# Acknowledgments

This report benefited from the support and assistance of many people in the Army and at RAND. We appreciate the support of our sponsor, GEN Dan K. Mc Neill, Commander of FORSCOM, and especially thank LTC Dan Haveman and others in the Homeland Defense Division for their good counsel and for the information they provided on the Army's response to Hurricane Katrina and on current planning for future domestic emergencies. We would like to thank those in the Defense Department, U.S. Northern Command (NORTHCOM), the National Guard Bureau, and the U.S. Army Center for Army Lessons Learned who provided us with background information on Hurricane Katrina. We also want to thank our RAND colleague Rick Brennan, who contributed to our research and analysis along the way, and to Jack Riley and Jim Carafano who provided thoughtful and careful reviews of an early draft of this work. Special thanks as well to our editor, Steve Kistler, whose careful review and revision greatly improved our monograph, and to Steve Bloodsworth, our terrific graphic artist. The content and conclusions of this work, however, remain solely the responsibility of the authors.

# Abbreviations

| | |
|---|---|
| AGR | Active Guard and Reserve |
| ARFORGEN | Army Force Generation |
| $C^2$ | command and control |
| CBRNE | chemical, biological, radiological, nuclear, and explosive |
| CERFP | CBRNE–Enhanced Force Packages |
| COCOM | combatant command |
| COORD | coordinated |
| CRAF | Civil Reserve Air Fleet |
| CSB | civil support battalion |
| CSIS | Center for Strategic and International Studies |
| DCO | Defense Coordinating Officer |
| DHS | Department of Homeland Security |
| DoD | Department of Defense |
| DSCA | Defense Support to Civil Authorities |
| EMAC | Emergency Management Assistance Compact |
| EOC | Emergency Operations Center |

| | |
|---|---|
| FCO | Federal Coordinating Officer |
| FEMA | Federal Emergency Management Agency |
| FORSCOM | U.S. Army Forces Command |
| HLS | homeland security |
| JCS | Joint Chiefs of Staff |
| JFCOM | Joint Forces Command |
| JFHQ | joint force headquarters |
| JFO | Joint Field Office |
| JTF | joint task force |
| LOEP | Louisiana Office of Emergency Preparedness |
| MP | Military Police |
| NGB | National Guard Bureau |
| NIMS | National Incident Management System |
| NORTHCOM | U.S. Northern Command |
| NRP | National Response Plan |
| OPCON | operational control |
| PFO | Principal Federal Officer |
| SJFHQ-CE | Standing Joint Force Headquarter-Command Element |
| TACON | tactical control |
| TAG | adjutant general |
| USAR | U.S. Army Reserves |
| WMD-CST | Weapons of Mass Destruction–Civil Support Team |

# CHAPTER ONE

# Introduction

## Background

Hurricane Katrina was one of the most catastrophic natural disasters ever to hit the United States. While 65 hurricanes of Category Three strength or higher made landfall in the United States between 1900 and 2000,[1] Hurricane Katrina stands out for several reasons. First, Hurricane Katrina was an extremely large storm, with hurricane force winds stretching 103 miles from its center[2] and tropical storm force winds extending 230 miles from its center.[3] As a result, Hurricane Katrina impacted 93,000 square miles of the United States.[4] At its peak, the storm's winds reached 175 mph.[5] Second, Hurricane Katrina produced an immense storm surge that exceeded 30 feet high in some places along the Gulf Coast and reached for miles inland. The surge was a particular problem in the city of New Orleans, parts of which are between one to ten feet below sea level. The levees protecting the city were quickly overwhelmed and failed, flooding about 80 percent

---

[1] Jerry D. Jarrell, Max Mayfield, Edward N. Rappaport, and Christopher W. Landsea, "The Deadliest, Costliest, and Most Intense United States Hurricanes from 1900 to 2000," National Oceanic and Atmospheric Administration Technical Memorandum NWS TPC-1, October 2001.

[2] The White House, *The Federal Response to Hurricane Katrina: Lessons Learned*, February 2006, p. 5.

[3] "New Orleans Braces for Monster Hurricane," CNN.com, August 29, 2005.

[4] The White House, *The Federal Response to Hurricane Katrina*, p. 5.

[5] National Hurricane Center, 11 AM Advisory, August 28, 2005.

of the city. As a result, Hurricane Katrina brought with it not only the problems that accompany a "typical" hurricane, but also an enormous flood in New Orleans.

In the end, Hurricane Katrina created over $96 billion in property damage, destroyed an estimated 300,000 homes, produced 118 million cubic yards of debris, displaced over 770,000 people, and killed an estimated 1,330 people. In comparison, Hurricane Andrew (one of the costliest U.S. natural disasters before Hurricane Katrina) created $33 billion in property damage, destroyed approximately 80,000 homes, produced 20 million cubic yards of debris, displaced approximately 250,000 people, and killed approximately 60 people. About 80 percent of the fatalities attributable to Hurricane Katrina occurred in the New Orleans metropolitan area; 231 fatalities occurred in Mississippi.[6] Figure 1.1 provides a comparison of the characteristics of Hurricane Katrina and Hurricane Andrew.

**Figure 1.1**
**Characteristics of Hurricane Andrew and Hurricane Katrina**

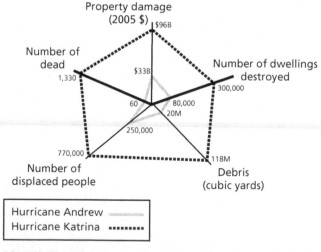

SOURCE: The White House, *The Federal Response to Hurricane Katrina: Lessons Learned,* February 2006, pp. 5–9.
RAND *MG603-1.1*

---

[6]   The White House, *The Federal Response to Hurricane Katrina*, pp. 7-8.

The nation's response to Hurricane Katrina was impressive. Figure 1.2 shows three representative statistics. The first is the cumulative number of people rescued by civilian and military responders at the end of four selected days, with a total of nearly 50,000 over the two weeks of the response. Second is the total number of people provided with emergency shelter at the end of each selected day, with nearly 250,000 at the peak of the response. The third is the cumulative number of people evacuated by the end of each selected day, with a total of nearly 80,000 over the course of the response. This number does not include those people who evacuated on their own and in advance of hurricane landfall.

**Figure 1.2**
**Accomplishments in Response to Hurricane Katrina**

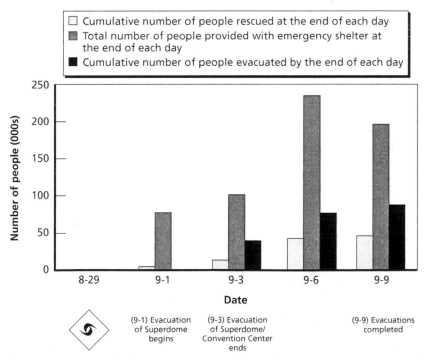

SOURCE: U.S. Department of Homeland Security, Situation Reports, August 29, 2005 through September 10, 2005.
RAND *MG603-1.2*

The magnitude of the response requirements encountered after Hurricane Katrina is similar to what the country might be faced with in a broad range of emergencies, both natural and man-made. Table 1.1 compares the effects and response requirements of Hurricane Katrina with what the Department of Homeland Security (DHS) Planning Scenarios see as the potential effects and response requirements of nuclear, radiological, and biological terrorist attacks and of a major earthquake.[7] Although Hurricane Katrina's death toll—over 1,300—makes it one of the deadlier hurricanes in U.S. history, the possible death tolls from nuclear and biological terrorist attacks could well be higher. In terms of possible destruction of infrastructure and utilities, Hurricane Katrina seems to be neither the highest nor the lowest; its effects are well within the range of what we might expect in these other types of domestic emergencies. While the requirement for the evacuation of about two million people during and after Hurricane Katrina seems higher than what would be expected following a terrorist attack, it is worth remembering that of those 2 million people, 1.2 million evacuated in the days before Hurricane Katrina made landfall.[8] Requirements for casualty care during the response to Hurricane Katrina were lower than the expected requirements of most of the terrorist attack scenarios and the earthquake shown in Table 1.1. It is reasonable to believe that the ample warning time prior to Hurricane Katrina's landfall and the extensive evacuations before the storm helped to keep the requirements for evacuation support lower than they might have been; this warning time also allowed state and local medical responders to prepare for the event. Not having such warning in the future could increase casualty-care requirements.

In summary, Hurricane Katrina provides a useful case study from which to draw lessons for the nation's and the Army's planning and

---

[7]    U.S. Department of Homeland Security, "National Planning Scenarios," Draft Version 20.2, April 2005.

[8]    See Johnny B. Bradberry, "Written Testimony of Johnny B. Bradberry, Secretary, La. Department of Transportation and Development Secretary," *Challenges in a Catastrophe: Evacuating New Orleans in Advance of Hurricane Katrina*, U.S. Senate Committee on Homeland Security and Governmental Affairs, January 31, 2006.

**Table 1.1**
**Effects and Requirements of Catastrophic Domestic Emergencies**

| | Hurricane Katrina | Radiological Attack | Nuclear Detonation | Biological Attack: Anthrax | Biological Attack: Plague | Natural Disaster: Major Earthquake |
|---|---|---|---|---|---|---|
| Description | | A dirty bomb containing cesium-137 is detonated in a moderate-to-large city | 10-kiloton improvised nuclear device is detonated in the business district of a large city | Aerosolized anthrax is released in a major urban area | Pneumonic plague bacteria is released in three main areas of a major city | An earthquake measuring 7.2 on the Richter scale hits a major metropolitan area and is followed by an 8.0 aftershock |
| Destruction | | | | | | |
| Fatalities | 1,349 | 180 | Widely variable; possibly tens of thousands | 13,000 | 2,500 | 1,400 |
| Infrastructure | 93,000 sq. miles | Transportation severely hampered by checkpoints; extensive contamination of about 36 city blocks | Total within radius of .5 to 1 mile; significant damage in larger area | Minimal damage | None | 150,000 buildings destroyed, 1 million damaged; significant transportation disruptions |
| Utilities | 2.5 million without power | Some damage near the explosion | Electrical power and tele-communications out for a couple of weeks; damaged in 3-mile radius | Minimal damage | No damage | Widespread water, gas, electricity, and communication outages |

**Table 1.1—Continued**

| | Hurricane Katrina | Radiological Attack | Nuclear Detonation | Biological Attack: Anthrax | Biological Attack: Plague | Natural Disaster: Major Earthquake |
|---|---|---|---|---|---|---|
| Requirements | | | | | | |
| Evacuations | 2,000,000 | Downwind populations | 450,000 or more | Possibly | Possibly | 300,000 households |
| Medical | Casualty care | Screening and decontaminating thousands of evacuees | Decontamination and short- and long-term care for tens of thousands | Care for over 325,000 exposures | Care for over 10,000 ill victims | Over 100,000 injuries, 18,000 hospitalizations; many medical facilities damaged |

SOURCES: For Hurricane Katrina, see The White House, *The Federal Response to Hurricane*; U.S. Senate, *Hurricane Katrina: A Nation Still Unprepared*, Report of the Committee on Homeland Security and Governmental Affairs, Washington, D.C.: U.S. Senate, May 6, 2002; U.S. House of Representatives, *A Failure of Initiative*, Final Report of the Select Bipartisan Committee to Investigate the Preparation and Response to Hurricane Katrina, Washington, D.C.: U.S. Government Printing Office, February 2006; U.S. Department of Homeland Security, "Highlights of United States Government Response to the Aftermath of Hurricane Katrina," press release, September 10, 2005; Senator John W. Warner, "Statement Made on the Senate Floor: DOD Hurricane Katrina Relief Efforts," September 15, 2005. For the scenarios, see U.S. Homeland Security Council, "Planning Scenarios: Executive Summaries," July 2004.

policies for the full range of catastrophic domestic emergencies that could arise within the United States.

## Analytical Approach

The problems encountered in the response to Hurricane Katrina were legion, as the many "lessons-learned" reports catalogue. Reports from the White House and Congress show the complex and diverse character of these problems, which ranged from ineffective planning processes in all levels of government—federal, state, and local—to mistakes in the coordination of operations across different levels of government, between military and civilian organizations, and among military units. Deficiencies in communications and the lack of information about what was happening were among the underlying reasons for poor coordination and planning. The congressional reports focus prominently on the lack of leadership, again at all levels of government.

Literally thousands of recommendations have been made by those investigating the response to Hurricane Katrina, and many steps have been taken or are under way that will improve the nation's plans and capabilities for responding to future catastrophic domestic emergencies. Many of these are tailored specifically to future hurricanes, but others are applicable to all types of potential domestic emergencies.

Underlying all of these lessons and recommendations is the assumption that had things been done differently in any given area, the response to Hurricane Katrina would have been more effective. Having researched what happened in detail, our own analysis of the nation's response to the storm began by looking for those problems that affected the outcome of the response in a major way (even though it is difficult to demonstrate a precise link between a single aspect of such a complex and enormous response and the characteristics of the outcome). We appreciate that the very nature of a catastrophic disaster will cause a gap between needs and resources, a gap that can never be totally eliminated.

The single largest problem encountered in the response to Hurricane Katrina was the speed with which civilian local, state, and federal government organizations were overwhelmed. The various lessons-learned reports cover in detail the lack of plans, deficiencies in certain types of response capabilities, and organizational inadequacies. However, the response was also affected in a major way by what the military was and was not able to accomplish in the critical first few days. The National Guard response was unprecedented in its size and quickness. Active-duty units from all the services responded, with the combined number of active and reserve forces growing to over 65,000 by the peak of response efforts. Nevertheless, the evacuations from the New Orleans Superdome and convention center were not completed until five days after hurricane landfall, and search and rescue operations across Louisiana and Mississippi were not finished until the end of the second week of the response. Therefore, our analysis focused on the considerations that influenced the timing and size of the deployments of the National Guard and active-duty forces and the lack of a unified command and control ($C^2$) structure for the military's response efforts. Drawing on the lessons learned in the military's response to Hurricane Katrina, we defined and analyzed the critical issues for future Army disaster response planning and operations.

One problem that was often raised in the lessons-learned reports is the lack of "situational awareness" during the Hurricane Katrina response,[9] so we asked: what kinds of information about the relief needs were available to officials from DHS, Joint Task Force (JTF)-Katrina, the Louisiana emergency offices, and other military staffs during the critical first few days after Hurricane Katrina made landfall? We discovered that there was considerable information about the dire straits of people and the significant destruction to infrastructure, enough information for officials to understand the capabilities required for an effective response. See the appendix for a description of our analysis and findings on situational awareness.

---

[9]  For example, the White House report states that the "lack of communications and situational awareness had a debilitating effect on the Federal response" and that the Secretary of Homeland Security "lacked real-time, accurate situational awareness." The White House, *The Federal Response to Hurricane Katrina*, pp. 50, 52.

## Report Organization

Chapter Two presents background information on how the nation is organized to respond to domestic emergencies and what happened during the nation's preparation and response to Hurricane Katrina. Chapter Three focuses on the critical problems that arose in the military during the response stage.[10] While there are lessons to be learned from all stages of such an event, we saw the utility in using the Hurricane Katrina response-stage case to help prepare for future situations that might arise with little or no warning. We also narrowed our focus to events in Mississippi and Louisiana, and then more specifically to the response in New Orleans. This sets the stage for Chapter Four, which offers our assessment of the implications of the Hurricane Katrina response effort for Army planning. This chapter outlines the changes that will need to be made to enable the military to respond more quickly and effectively to such events in the future. Chapter Five presents our conclusions and recommendations, and the Appendix provides our findings as to the types of information that were available to decisionmakers across the government as they developed the response to Hurricane Katrina.

The study benefited from the many lessons-learned reports that have been produced by organizations throughout the government, as well as from the hours of congressional testimony of participants in the Hurricane Katrina response. We also received copies of the daily briefings that senior officials were given over the course of the response. These briefings were given to officials from DHS and the Federal Emergency Management Agency (FEMA); the offices of the Secretary of Defense, the Joint Staff, and the Department of the Army; in the U.S. Department of Defense (DoD) U.S. Northern Command (NORTHCOM), U.S. Forces Command (FORSCOM), and JTF-Katrina; the

---

[10] In the case of a hurricane, there is time for preparations. After landfall, there is a period—often referred to as the response stage—that includes initial search and rescue operations, the provision of relief supplies, and the restoration of various types of infrastructure. This period is followed by the recovery stage, when civilian agencies and private sector groups commence long-term reconstruction. Some would argue that in the case of a hurricane (when warning is available), the response stage actually begins prior to hurricane landfall.

National Guard Bureau (NGB); and the governor's and emergency offices in Louisiana.

In this book, we use the acronym HLS (homeland security) to denote military activities in support of civilian organizations, i.e., those involved in preventing and responding to terrorist attacks as well as in responding to other kinds of domestic emergencies, including natural disasters and civil disturbances. This is a broader definition of HLS than is found in *National Strategy for Homeland Security*, which focuses only on counterterrorism within the United States.[11] Our definition of HLS encompasses what DoD, in its *Strategy for Homeland Defense and Civil Support*, calls Defense Support of Civil Authorities (DSCA) and what Joint Publication 1-02, *The Department of Defense Dictionary of Military and Associated Terms*, defines as civil support ("Department of Defense support to U.S. civil authorities for domestic emergencies, and for designated law enforcement and other activities").[12]

---

[11]   Office of Homeland Security, *National Strategy for Homeland Security*, July 2002, p. 2.

[12]   U.S. Department of Defense, *Strategy for Homeland Defense and Civil Support*, Washington, D.C.: U.S. Department of Defense, June 2005; Joint Publication 1-02, *The Department of Defense Dictionary of Military and Associated Terms*, Washington, D.C.: Joint Staff, April 12, 2001, as ammended through March 22, 2007.

# CHAPTER TWO

# Background

## How the Nation Is Organized to Respond to Domestic Emergencies

Responding to domestic emergencies within the United States is primarily the purview of local and state governments, both by design and in how the nation has responded to such events historically. The federal government plays a supporting role, recognizing that local and state governments are in the best position to understand the needs of their citizens and to respond quickly. For those things that states and localities cannot accomplish, the nation turns to civilian and then military organizations in the federal government. In the case of major domestic emergencies, the federal role has been critical, but it has always been supplementary to local and state resources.

DHS was established by Congress in 2002, and in 2003 it assumed primary control of federal activities related to disaster management. FEMA, which became a part of DHS in 2003, is the primary agency tasked with the coordination of federal disaster assistance. FEMA is not, for the most part, an operational provider of assistance. Rather, FEMA's main role is to manage the response efforts of the rest of the federal government.[1]

The nation's planning and response to natural and man-made disasters is outlined in the National Response Plan (NRP), which DHS

---

[1] The White House, *The Federal Response to Hurricane Katrina*, p. 16.

released in 2004 and revised in the aftermath of Hurricane Katrina.[2] The NRP, consistent with the U.S. Constitution, recognizes that planning and preparing for and responding to natural and other disasters are primarily responsibilities of the states. Local authorities request assistance from the state if local resources are overwhelmed, and state officials request assistance from the federal government if the state government is in turn overwhelmed.

The NRP is based on the National Incident Management System (NIMS), which outlines a consistent framework for incident management across the country, regardless of the level of government. The central component of the NIMS is the Incident Command System, which provides the means to coordinate a response through five major functional areas: Command, Planning, Operations, Logistics, and Finance/Administration.[3] The Incident Command System is flexible and scalable enough to coordinate the response to any size disaster, and it helps to maintain common terminology and chains of command to avoid confusion or overlap in response efforts among agencies and individuals. In addition, the NRP uses the Emergency Support Function framework, which divides topical responsibilities into at least 15 areas.[4] Taken as a whole, the NRP and the NIMS present a unified command structure for dealing with all hazards—both man-made and natural—across local, state, and federal jurisdictions.

The NRP also provides a Principal Federal Officer (PFO), appointed by the Secretary of Homeland Security, to coordinate overall

---

[2] See U.S. Department of Homeland Security, *National Response Plan*, December 2004, and U.S. Department of Homeland Security, *Notice of Change to the National Response Plan*, May 25, 2006.

[3] U.S. Department of Homeland Security, *National Incident Management System*, March 1, 2004, p. 7.

[4] The Emergency Support Functions are ESF#1: Transportation; ESF#2: Communications; ESF#3: Public Works and Engineering; ESF#4: Firefighting; ESF#5: Emergency Management; ESF#6: Mass Care, Housing and Human Services; ESF#7: Resource Support; ESF#8: Public Health and Medical Services; ESF#9: Urban Search and Rescue; ESF#10: Oil and Hazardous Materials Response: ESF#11; Agriculture and Natural Resources; ESF#12: Energy; ESF#13: Public Safety and Security; ESF#14: Long-Term Community Recovery and Mitigation; ESF#15: External Affairs (DHS, *National Response Plan*, p. xii).

federal incident management and assistance activities across the spectrum of prevention, preparedness, response, and recovery.[5] However, the PFO does not direct or replace the incident command structure established at the incident, nor does the PFO have directive authority over other federal officials. The primary piece of federal legislation covering the provision of federal disaster aid is the Robert T. Stafford Disaster Relief and Emergency Assistance Act. The Stafford Act reiterates the philosophy that in a disaster, local resources should be used first, then state resources, and finally federal resources. The Stafford Act also outlines the process by which state governors can request assistance from the federal government. The NRP stipulates that a Federal Coordinating Officer (FCO) is responsible for managing and coordinating federal resource activities related to Stafford Act disasters.[6]

The Joint Field Office (JFO) is a temporary federal facility established locally at the time of a disaster to coordinate operational federal assistance activities to the affected areas. The JFO is responsible for providing a common operating picture to all federal agencies.[7] If DoD appoints a Defense Coordinating Officer (DCO) in an emergency, this person serves as DoD's single point of contact at the JFO.[8]

The NRP distinguishes between incident responses that require management by the Secretary of Homeland Security—termed Incidents of National Significance—and the majority of incident responses, which are handled by states and local authorities.[9] There is also a Catastrophic Incident Annex to the NRP; this annex addresses no-notice or

---

[5]   DHS *National Response Plan*, p. 33.

[6]   DHS, *National Response Plan*, p. 33. In 2006, the National Response Plan was changed in order to provide the Secretary with the ability, during incidents other than terrorism, to combine the roles of the PFO and FCO. DHS, *Notice of Change to the National Response Plan*, p. 6.

[7]   DHS, *National Response Plan*, p. 16. In the May 25, 2006, *Notice of Change to the National Response Plan* there is a call for the collocation of DoD Joint Task Force headquarters with the PFO at the JFO whenever possible. DHS, *Notice of Change to the National Response Plan*, p. 6.

[8]   DHS, *National Response Plan*, p. 37.

[9]   DHS, *Notice of Change to the National Response Plan*, p. 14.

short-notice incidents of catastrophic size for which anticipatory planning and prepositioning is precluded.[10]

Military forces are often called upon to respond to disasters and emergency situations, as they offer a large number of readily accessible personnel and have preexisting control structures and communications and transportation assets. In the aftermath of Hurricane Katrina, both active-duty and National Guard forces assisted response efforts in various capacities. The following provides a simplified overview of how military forces can be accessed and used in such situations.[11]

## Active-Duty Military

Active-duty military forces fall under the command of the President of the United States and are available to support state and local civil authorities. There are, however, some restrictions on the role of federal troops in certain situations. In particular, federal troops are subject to the Posse Comitatus Act of 1878, which restricts their involvement in law-enforcement activities.[12] Even when federal troops are used to sup-

---

[10] DHS, *Notice of Change to the National Response Plan*, p. 6.

[11] Current federal law generally forbids the use of the U.S. Army Reserve (USAR) for missions within the United States, and given the existing requirements for overseas operations, these forces were for the most part not called upon to respond to Hurricane Katrina. Until 2002, Section 12304 of Title 10 contained an express restriction on the authority of the Secretary of Defense to call members or units of the federal reserve components to active duty to execute provisions of the Insurrection Statutes or to otherwise "provide assistance to either the Federal Government or a State in time of a serious natural or man-made disaster, accident, or catastrophe." The rationale for that prohibition was that the National Guard is the appropriate entity for such purposes, including activities following its call to federal service. Section 514 of the National Defense Authorization Act for Fiscal Year 2003 expanded the authority for a reserve call-up under section 12304 to include "a terrorist attack or threatened terrorist attack in the United States that results, or could result, in catastrophic loss of life or property." The House-Senate conference on the National Defense Authorization Act for Fiscal Year 2004 substituted the word "significant" for "catastrophic," with the result being an even-further expansion of the federal government's authority to respond to most terrorist incidents. Gary Cecchine et al., *Triage for Civil Support: Using Military Medical Assets to Respond to Terrorist Attacks*, Santa Monica, Calif.: RAND Corporation, MG-217-OSD, 2004.

[12] The restrictions of the Posse Comitatus Act and related legislation are complicated and often subject to interpretation. For background on these issues, see Lynn E. Davis et al., *Army Forces for Homeland Security*, Santa Monica, Calif.: RAND Corporation, MG-221-A, 2004,

port state or local governments, they still receive federal pay and benefits. As with other federal assets, active-duty military forces are generally called upon to respond to domestic disasters only when local and state assets, including the National Guard, are overwhelmed.

## The National Guard

National Guard forces fall under the command of the governor of the state or territory in which they are based. Governors can call National Guard forces to state active duty to provide assistance during disasters. The National Guard forces remain under the control of the governor and are generally paid by their state or territory, although there is provision under Title 32 of the U.S. Code for the federal government to pay the costs of National Guard forces operating under the control of their governor. When Guard forces receive pay and benefits from the federal government but remain under the control of the governor, they are not subject to the Posse Comitatus Act and so can perform law-enforcement duties.

National Guard forces can be federalized under Title 10 of the U.S. Code. In this case, the president, not the governor, controls Guard forces, and they receive federal pay and benefits like their active-duty counterparts. However, they are also subject to the restrictions imposed by the Posse Comitatus Act and, therefore, cannot normally perform law-enforcement duties within the United States.

## How the Nation Prepared and Responded to Hurricane Katrina

Before Hurricane Katrina made landfall, response preparations were made in the states and across the federal government. For the most part, these preparations followed plans that were already in place; their

---

pp. 59–67; and U.S. Government Accountability Office, *Homeland Defense: DOD Needs to Assess the Structure of U.S. Forces for Domestic Military Missions*, GAO-03-670, Washington, D.C.: U.S. Government Accountability Office, July 2003.

characteristics are reported in detail in the various lessons-learned reports.[13]

The story of Hurricane Katrina began on Tuesday, August 23, 2005, when the National Hurricane Center announced that tropical depression 12 had formed over the southeastern Bahamas, with maximum sustained winds near 35 mph. The DoD conducted an inventory of its response capabilities and established a "crisis action cell" to allow for rapid processing of FEMA requests. FEMA activated its hurricane liaison team, and NORTHCOM issued its first warning orders to Regional Emergency Preparedness Liaison Officers, State Emergency Preparedness Officers, and the Senior Army Advisors (National Guard) in the states expected to be affected. As the hurricane turned toward New Orleans on Friday, August 26, Louisiana Governor Kathleen Blanco activated Louisiana's Emergency Operations Center (EOC) and declared a state of emergency.[14] Governor Haley Barbour did the same in Mississippi.[15] Both states also began activating their National Guards. NORTHCOM issued an execute order, setting initial DoD relief actions into motion. The next day, evacuations began in New Orleans, FEMA teams were deployed, and Governor Blanco wrote a letter to President Bush requesting that he declare a state of emergency for Louisiana, thus releasing the federal aid provided for under the Stafford Act.

This same day, President Bush officially declared a state of emergency in Louisiana and ordered federal aid to begin flowing to the state. The next day, Sunday, August 28, he did the same for Mississippi. FEMA Director Michael Brown deployed to Louisiana, DCOs deployed to Mississippi and Louisiana, and lead elements of what would become JTF-Katrina moved into Mississippi.

---

[13] Our chronology of events draws upon The White House, *The Federal Response to Hurricane Katrina*; U.S. Senate, *Hurricane Katrina: A Nation Still Unprepared*; U.S. House, *A Failure of Initiative*.

[14] Louisiana Office of the Governor, *Proclamation No. 48 KBB 2005*, Baton Rouge, La., August 26, 2005; U.S. House, *A Failure of Initiative*, p. 64.

[15] Haley Barbour, Governor of Mississippi, *Executive Order No. 939*, August 26, 2005; U.S. House, *A Failure of Initiative*, p. 60.

At 7:00 AM EDT on August 29, Hurricane Katrina made landfall near Buras, Louisiana, as a very strong Category Three storm. Accounts vary as to when the levees surrounding New Orleans were breached or overtopped, but as early as 9:12 AM EDT, the National Weather Service received a report of a levee breach and shortly thereafter issued a flash flood warning. Mid-morning, President Bush declared Louisiana, Mississippi, and Alabama federal disaster areas.

With dawn the day after the storm came the realization of how extensive the devastation was. Later that day, Secretary of Homeland Security Michael Chertoff declared Hurricane Katrina to be an Incident of National Significance and appointed Michael Brown as the PFO. LTG Russel Honoré was designated as commander of JTF-Katrina. On that same day, thousands of National Guard forces began flowing into Mississippi and Louisiana, with about 45,000 in the region by the end of the second week of the response.

On the third day after hurricane landfall, September 1, 2005, the evacuation of the New Orleans Superdome began; two days later, the evacuations of the Superdome and the convention center were complete. That day, September 3, President Bush ordered the deployment of 7,200 active-duty Army and Marine land forces to Louisiana to support the ongoing search and rescue operations and the provision of relief supplies. In the next week, Deputy Secretary of Defense Gordon England signed a memorandum approving the use of Title 32 funds to support Hurricane Katrina disaster relief efforts, making their applicability retroactive to the date of Hurricane landfall. By September 10, all the evacuations had been completed and major aid and reconstruction efforts were under way. The recovery stage had begun.

# CHAPTER THREE

# The Military Response to Hurricane Katrina

Military forces played a critical role in the nation's response to Hurricane Katrina, so we initially focused our research on the timeliness and robustness of the deployments of the National Guard and active-duty forces, as well as on the characteristics of the military $C^2$ structure used during the response. We looked for the lessons to be learned, highlighting both accomplishments and problems.

## The National Guard Response

State governors have a long history of calling on their National Guard to respond to domestic emergencies. The response of the National Guard in Hurricane Katrina is praised for its size and comprehensiveness in the various lessons-learned reports issued to date.[1] It is criticized for its perceived slowness in the House lessons-learned report, "fragmented deployment system" in the White House report, and for its lack of coordination with other military responses in the Senate report.[2] What were the considerations that influenced the size and timing of the National Guard response?

The governors of Louisiana and Mississippi began mobilizing their Army and Air National Guard in advance of Hurricane Katrina's land-

---

[1]  U.S. Senate, *Hurricane Katrina*, Chapter 26.

[2]  U.S. House, *A Failure of Initiative*, p. 205; The White House, *The Federal Response to Hurricane Katrina*, p. 43; U.S. Senate, *Hurricane Katrina*, pp. 26–50.

fall.[3] As Table 3.1 indicates, by hurricane landfall, almost all available Louisiana National Guard forces were called up to state active duty. The size of the mobilization effected by the Louisiana governor was smaller than it might have been, as Louisiana had a brigade combat team mobilized and in the process of redeploying from Iraq.[4] Of those available in Mississippi, a much smaller number were called up;[5] Mississippi also had a brigade combat team redeploying from Iraq at the time the storm hit.

Figures 3.1 and 3.2 show the buildup in Mississippi and Louisiana of Army National Guard forces over the first week of the response, showing both those from Louisiana and Mississippi and those from other states that were operating through the Emergency Management

**Table 3.1**
**Availability and Utilization of Louisiana and Mississippi Army and Air National Guard**

| National Guard | Louisiana | Mississippi |
|---|---|---|
| Total number | 10,225 | 11,925 |
| Number redeploying from Iraq | 3,800 | 2,700 |
| Number available to governor (August 2005) | 6,425 | 9,225 |
| Number employed in Hurricane Katrina response | 5,700 | 2,941 |

SOURCES: Information on the number of National Guard personnel by state and those employed in Hurricane Katrina provided by the National Guard Bureau. The number redeploying from Iraq found in: U.S. Army, Headquarters Department of the Army (G-3) "Katrina Update," briefing, September 1, 2005.

---

[3] According to the White House report, three days before landfall some 2,000 personnel were activated in Louisiana and 750 in Mississippi. The White House, *The Federal Response to Hurricane Katrina*, p. 24.

[4] U.S. Army, Headquarters Department of the Army (G-3), "Katrina Update," briefing, September 1, 2005.

[5] The source of this information is the National Guard Bureau. Media reports suggest that guardsmen in Mississippi who had lost their homes were exempt. See Ann Scott Tyson, "Strain of Iraq War Means the Relief Burden Will Have to Be Shared," *Washington Post*, August 31, 2005, p. A14.

**Figure 3.1**
**Army National Guard Buildup in Mississippi**

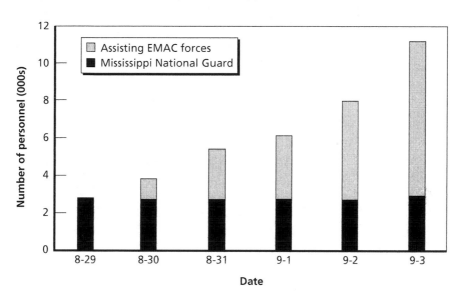

SOURCE: U.S. Army, Institute of Land Warfare, "Natural Disaster Response: Hurricane Katrina," briefing, October 5, 2005.
RAND *MG603-3.1*

Assistance Compact (EMAC).[6] On the day Hurricane Katrina made landfall, there were over 4,700 Army National Guard personnel operating in Louisiana and some 2,700 operating in Mississippi.

Army National Guard units from other states augmented the Louisiana and Mississippi Army National Guard, and by the end of the first week of the response, over 15,000 Army National Guard troops were on the ground in Louisiana and over 11,000 were on the ground in Mississippi. The flow of Army National Guard personnel into Mississippi was quicker than into Louisiana. Not until the end of the first

---

[6] The EMAC is a mutual assistance agreement among the states for providing civilian and military assistance. EMAC came into being in 1996. See Public Law 104-321. It is administered by the National Emergency Management Association. It is not a part of the federal government but is an agreement among 49 states, the District of Columbia, Puerto Rico, and the Virgin Islands to provide assistance across state lines when a disaster occurs. Hawaii is the only state that is not a member. The governor of the affected area must first declare a state of emergency, and then that state must request the help it needs. Protocols allow reimbursement to all assisting states, and EMAC has procedures to resolve liability issues.

**Figure 3.2**
**Army National Guard Buildup in Louisiana**

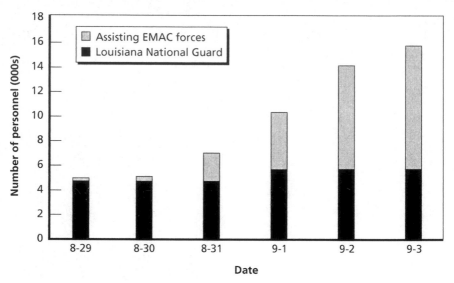

SOURCE: U.S. Army, Institute of Land Warfare, "Natural Disaster Response: Hurricane Katrina," briefing, October 5, 2005.
RAND *MG603-3.2*

week did the number in Louisiana exceed that in Mississippi, although it eventually grew to more than twice the number in Mississippi.

A week later, on September 9, the numbers had grown to over 41,000 Army National Guard personnel in Mississippi and Louisiana. They came from 45 states plus the District of Columbia, the Virgin Islands, and Puerto Rico. Four additional states eventually sent troops as well. In addition, some 3,000 Army National Guard forces supported the operations in Mississippi and Louisiana from outside the states, including forces from Alabama and Florida. In this same period, the number of Air National Guard personnel in Mississippi and Louisiana grew from just over 400 to almost 4,000.

The National Guard response was unprecedented, both its overall size and the speed with which the units arrived. Before Hurricane Katrina, the largest domestic National Guard deployment was 16,599 troops in support of the response to the San Francisco earthquake of

1989. These troops were mostly from California and were called up to state active duty by the governor over a three-month period.[7]

In the response to Hurricane Katrina, the adjutants general (TAGs) of Louisiana and Mississippi initially requested assistance from National Guard units from other states through the EMAC. While the response to these requests was initially slowed by the loss of communication caused by the storm, over 2,000 resource requests were filled through EMAC during the Hurricane Katrina response.[8]

Mississippi asked for security assistance, engineering support, and helicopters.[9] Louisiana requested the same, adding requests for aviation and ground units.[10] Then, given the catastrophic damage and the overwhelming need for assistance, both states issued a more general call for assistance.[11]

At the request of the Louisiana TAG, the NGB began to coordinate the response in both Louisiana and Mississippi.[12] In a videoconference with many of the TAGs across the nation on Wednesday,

---

[7]   See Chief of the National Guard Bureau, *Annual Review*, 1990, p. 82.

[8]   U.S. House, *A Failure of Initiative*, p. 144. According to the DHS Office of the Inspector General, the majority of the EMAC assistance was for National Guard resources and law enforcement personnel, though there were other types: medical teams, search and rescue teams, and commodities. U.S. Department of Homeland Security, Office of the Inspector General, *A Performance Review of FEMA's Disaster Management Activities in Response to Hurricane Katrina*, March 2006, p. 17.

[9]   U.S. House, *A Failure of Initiative*, pp. 59, 61, 66–67.

[10]   U.S. House, *A Failure of Initiative*, p. 66; Louisiana Office of the Governor, "Overview of Governor Kathleen Babineaux Blanco's Actions in Preparation For and Response to Hurricane Katrina," Response to U.S. Senate Committee on Homeland Security and Governmental Affairs Document and Information Request Dated October 7, 2005 and to the U.S. House of Representatives Select Committee to Investigate the Preparation for and Response to Hurricane Katrina, December 2, 2005.

[11]   U.S. House, *A Failure of Initiative*, p. 227. The House report (pp. 144–145) views the EMAC process as a success, but along with other reports focused on the need for better coordination of the EMAC and NGB processes and for streamlining the approval process. According to U.S. Senate, *Hurricane Katrina*, Chapter 26-49 "the EMAC process proved neither suitable nor capable to handle the type of large scale deployment of military troops that were needed in the Gulf region."

[12]   Louisiana Office of the Governor, "Overview of Governor Kathleen Babineaux Blanco's Actions."

August 31, LTG H. Steven Blum, Director of NGB, solicited assistance and decided not to worry about the authorizing paperwork.[13]

In a follow-on message, General Blum requested "maximum support from all States to mitigate the loss of life and limb in support of Louisiana and Mississippi." The message went on to describe the concept of operations and $C^2$ arrangements. It announced the sending of the 35th and 38th National Guard Division headquarters to the region, and then described the units that would deploy within the next 24 to 72 hours "to save human life, prevent immediate human suffering, or lessen major property damage or destruction." Along with Mississippi and Louisiana National Guard troops, the message projected that roughly 10,000 National Guard troops from other states would be in Mississippi and Louisiana by the end of the day and another 10,000 two days later.[14]

These units mostly consisted of Military Police (MP) and security forces, with transportation, aviation, and engineer units also included for Louisiana. In the days following General Blum's message, the daily briefings to the director of the NGB provided an accounting of what each state was sending, what units and personnel had arrived in Louisiana and Mississippi along with a description of their missions. The briefings also included projections of forces that would be arriving over each of the following days. These projections turned out to be high for the first four days but became fairly accurate thereafter.

Although National Guard units from outside states deployed to Louisiana and Mississippi as a result of EMAC requests and personal conversations between the TAGs and between governors across the states, the units sent largely consisted of the types considered "likely to be required" by the outside the states.[15] There was no attempt to use

---

[13] U.S. House, *A Failure of Initiative*, 2006, p. 212.

[14] See National Guard Bureau, cable to state adjutants general, August 31, 2005; U.S. Department of Defense, Press Briefing, August 31, 2005.

[15] U.S. House, *A Failure of Initiative*, 2006, p. 205, based on a written response from LTG H. Steven Blum, states: "Initially, this operated via a 'push' methodology with supporting states pushing available forces based on requirements identified by the Adjutants General in the supported states."

the process known in the military as "troops-to-task analysis." According to the Senate report, most National Guard troops dispatched to Louisiana did not know what the mission would be or where it would be performed until they arrived.[16]

Once in the states, the units undertook a range of tasks: evacuation assistance, search and rescue, security, commodity (water, food, and ice) and fuel distribution, medical care, restoration of communications, law-enforcement support, debris removal, and the rebuilding of damaged infrastructure.

The types of units in Louisiana and Mississippi at the end of the second week of the response are shown in Figure 3.3. Most consisted of general purpose forces, but there were also engineer, aviation, medical, and $C^2$ units. Among the specialized types of units sent were the

**Figure 3.3**
**Types of Army National Guard Personnel (September 9, 2005)**

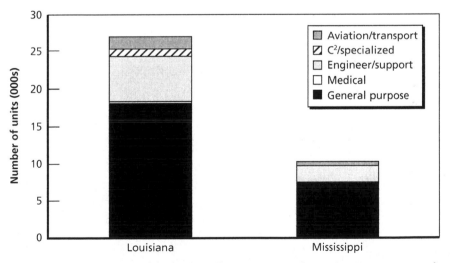

SOURCE: National Guard Bureau, GIS Staff, "Army National Guard Units in Support of Hurricane Disaster Area, Mississippi and Louisiana," September 9, 2005.
RAND MG603-3.3

---

[16] U.S. Senate, *Hurricane Katrina*, Chapter 26-53.

Weapons of Mass Destruction–Civil Support Teams (WMD-CSTs), special teams designed to respond to incidents involving weapons of mass destruction. These teams also include an emergency communications suite. Four days after hurricane landfall WMD-CST teams from nine states and the District of Columbia were on their way to Louisiana and Mississippi.[17]

The units that arrived were for the most part the types of forces needed to assist in the response efforts. Only in the case of MP units were deficiencies sufficient to affect operations. In a DoD briefing, General Blum reported that, while eventually successful, National Guard forces were not able to assume control of the New Orleans convention center until five days after hurricane landfall because of the time required to amass the necessary forces.[18] MP deficiencies arose even though the initial Mississippi and Louisiana EMAC requests were specifically for security and law-enforcement units, and two days after landfall, 4,200 MPs were deploying to the region.[19] Looking back, General Blum also stated that he wished that he had been quicker to move the $C^2$ elements of the National Guard division headquarters.[20]

The National Guard's ability to respond to Hurricane Katrina with the necessary types of units in a timely fashion was affected by a number of factors. One was the generalized call for help that went out after the first few days. In the absence of requests for specific types of units, any units that were available were viewed as needed.

Second, not all of each state's National Guard units were available. Some were federalized under Title 10 (e.g., units involved in operations in Iraq and Afghanistan) or conducting domestic operations under Title 32 (e.g., units involved in counterdrug operations).

---

[17] U.S. House, *A Failure of Initiative*, p. 229.

[18] U.S. Department of Defense, Press Briefing, September 3, 2005.

[19] U.S. Senate, *Hurricane Katrina*, Chapter 26-58. According to LTG Blum, the disintegration of the civilian police force in New Orleans was not anticipated. DoD, Press Briefing, September 3, 2005.

[20] U.S. Senate, *Hurricane Katrina*, Chapter 26-54.

The percentage "available" varied by state, but the average was about 75 percent.[21]

Third, the National Guard response from states outside the disaster area consisted for the most part of volunteers, though there were reports of some governors calling some soldiers to involuntary state active duty to fill out units. Across the states, the National Guard response averaged about 15 percent of "available" troops. There do not appear to have been instances in which governors felt any need to hold back units for other potential emergencies within their states.

Fourth, the speed with which National Guard units arrived in the region was a function of the time required for guardsmen to gather into units and deploy. According to the Center for Army Lessons Learned report, units with well-rehearsed plans were able to deploy within 24 hours of notification and move hundreds of miles with little advance coordination. Others suffered time lags in building up and moving as a coherent unit.[22] In deploying to Mississippi and Louisiana, National Guard units used both ground and air (commercial and military) transport, with about the same number of personnel traveling by air as by ground. The units that responded initially and the smaller units tended to come by air, although no clear pattern emerged.[23]

Notwithstanding the National Guard's impressive response, the evacuation of the Superdome did not begin until the third day after Hurricane Katrina made landfall, and the evacuations of the Superdome and the convention center were not completed until two days later.

The National Guard response might have been more effective had unit types been matched to specific missions and needs. However, had this been attempted, the arrival of units could well have been delayed

---

[21] We drew these figures from analyzing the percentages available by state, which were provided by the NGB. An NGB briefing dated August 31, 2005, identified about 75,500 Army National Guard as "currently mobilized." Another 38,000 were "alerted" or "pending alert." If all these are assumed to be unavailable, the percentage drops to below 70 percent.

[22] U.S. Army, Center for Army Lessons Learned, *Disaster Response Hurricanes Katrina and Rita Initial Impressions Report*, 2005, p. 15.

[23] This analysis was based on information in U.S. Army, "Natural Disaster Response: Hurricane Katrina."

pending an assessment of the situation. Moving more of the units by air or having military air transport available might also have made the response quicker, though how much so is not clear given the destruction of airfields in the region.

As noted earlier, those National Guard units that came from outside Louisiana and Mississippi mostly consisted of volunteers. The response could have been more robust if the governors of states other than Mississippi and Louisiana had been prepared to call up more guardsmen to state active duty on an involuntary basis. However, in so doing they would have reduced the number of units available in their own states were another disaster to strike. Had the emergency been a terrorist attack, particularly one involving weapons of mass destruction, it is possible that governors would have been willing to offer up even fewer of their National Guard units because of concern about the potential danger of follow-on attacks in their own states. In such a case, guardsmen, too, could be reluctant to volunteer for duty in the immediate aftermath of an attack, particularly duty that would take them far away from home.

Given all of these factors, the Hurricane Katrina case suggests that the size and timeliness of the National Guard response to the storm may be about what the nation can expect in future catastrophic domestic emergencies, given current capabilities and planning assumptions.

## The Response of Active-Duty Forces

Active-duty forces have historically been called upon to respond to major domestic emergencies, and before Hurricane Katrina made landfall, aviation units were alerted and the JTF-Katrina was formed. By the end of the second week of the response, there were over 20,000 active-duty personnel involved in relief operations in Mississippi and Louisiana. The lessons-learned reports praise the contribution of the active-duty forces, with only the Senate report questioning the delay in the deployment of active-duty land forces.[24] The timing and size of the active-duty response was influenced by a number of factors.

Immediately after hurricane landfall, a variety of Army, Navy, Marine, and Air Force active-duty units responded. The U.S. Transportation Command flew in swift-water rescue teams. The Army Corps of Engineers, which in the NRP has the lead for public works and engineering, began contracting for the provision of water, ice, emergency power, and the removal of debris.[25] In addition, the Corps of Engineers was immediately engaged with the National Guard in efforts to repair the levees surrounding New Orleans. A Marine Amphibious Readiness Group loaded with disaster response equipment prepared to sail for the region, as did a naval hospital ship.[26] The flow of active-duty forces from different military services into Louisiana and Mississippi, along with the National Guard, is shown in Figure 3.4.[27] For the first five days, the active-duty forces came almost entirely from the Navy, Marines, and Air Force.

The initial active force response focused on search and rescue operations and primarily involved helicopter units. Although Coast Guard helicopters were the first to respond, beginning operations as soon as the hurricane had passed over, Air Force and National Guard helicopters were also soon on the scene. The helicopter-carrier *USS Bataan* was in port in Texas and began to steam toward the region behind the hurricane. Its aircraft began search and rescue missions the day after landfall. Marine and active-duty Army helicopters were deployed the next day, with the Marines coming from the Second Marine Expedi-

---

[24] U.S. Senate, *Hurricane Katrina*, Chapter 26.

[25] U.S. House, *A Failure of Initiative*, p. 217.

[26] See U.S. Department of Homeland Security, "United States Government Response to the Aftermath of Hurricane Katrina," press release, August 31, 2005.

[27] Senator John Warner catalogued the details of the DoD deployment at its peak: 20 ships; 346 helicopters; 68 fixed wing aircraft; and 72,614 active duty troops, reservists, and National Guardsmen (Senator John Warner, "Additional Views of Senator John Warner, Senate Committee on Homeland Security and Governmental Affairs, Hurricane Katrina Report," May 9, 2006).

**Figure 3.4**
**Flow of Military Forces to Mississippi and Louisiana**

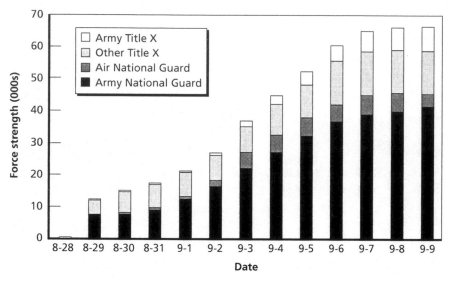

SOURCE: U.S. Army, Institute of Land Warfare, "Natural Disaster Response: Hurricane Katrina," briefing, October 5, 2005; National Guard Bureau Battle Update Briefings; U.S. Department of Defense, Office of the Assistant Secretary of Defense (Public Affairs), press briefings, August, 31 and September 2, 6, and 9, 2005; JTF-Katrina Commander's Assessments (J-1 PERSTATS).
RAND *MG603-3.4*

tionary Force and the Army coming from the First Air Cavalry Brigade at Fort Hood.[28]

In terms of the types of Army units, the initial deployments involved headquarters staffs, aviation, and the Corps of Engineers. See Figure 3.5.

The question arises as to why the decision to deploy active-duty Army and Marine land forces was not made until five days after hurricane landfall, even though both the Army and the Marines have units in a ready status for responding to civil disturbances and for unforeseen contingencies at home and overseas.

---

[28] See U.S. Department of Defense, "Special Defense Department Briefing with Commander of Joint Task Force Katrina," transcript, September 1, 2005; U.S. Senate, *Hurricane Katrina*, Chapter 12-31. DoD issued its first official orders for military support (in the form of helicopters) the evening of hurricane landfall.

**Figure 3.5**
**Buildup of Army Active-Duty Units**

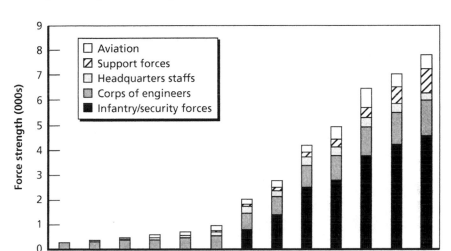

SOURCE: JTF-Katrina Commander's Daily Assessments (J-1 PERSTATS).
RAND *MG603-3.5*

Prior to Hurricane Katrina's landfall, Governor Blanco of Louisiana stated in a letter to the president that the severity of the incident was going to require supplemental federal assistance. The letter included general estimates of the kinds of federal civilian assistance she thought would be needed but did not include a request for military assistance.[29] The president acted on this request by declaring a state of emergency in Louisiana. The Governor of Mississippi also asked for federal assistance in advance of hurricane landfall, and the president declared a state of emergency there as well.[30]

---

[29] See letters from Governor Kathleen Babineaux Blanco of Louisiana to the President of United States, August 27, 2005, and August 28, 2005. According to the Senate report, the DCO in Louisiana received no specific requests from the Louisiana National Guard prior to hurricane landfall. U.S. Senate, *Hurricane Katrina*, Chapter 26-16.

[30] According to the Senate report, preparations for Hurricane Katrina did not include efforts on the part of either FEMA or DHS leadership to engage DoD to learn what specific capabilities it might be able to provide in advance of hurricane landfall, or to seek to call upon DoD support capabilities. U.S. Senate, *Hurricane Katrina*, Chapter 12-24.

On the afternoon Hurricane Katrina made landfall, Governor Blanco called President Bush asking for help: "we need everything you've got."[31] The next day, August 30, JTF-Katrina was established under the command of LTG Russel Honoré, Commander of the U.S. First Army. MG Bennett C. Landreneau, the Louisiana TAG, has testified that on that day he conveyed the governor's request to General Honoré for significant federal military assistance including troops.[32] He also said that he asked for an Army division headquarters to plan and coordinate the evacuation of New Orleans.[33]

In a call to the president the following day, August 31, Governor Blanco asked for assistance from federal troops.[34] When General Honoré arrived later that day, Governor Blanco learned that he had with him only a small staff. In a second call to President Bush, she estimated that she would need 40,000 troops.[35] On the same day Assistant Secretary of Defense for Homeland Defense Paul McHale said that DoD had units on alert for the restoration of civil order, but he did not anticipate having to use them.[36] Nevertheless, late the same day, FORSCOM ordered the Army to "be prepared to provide a brigade size force to operate distribution centers, and/or if appropriate autho-

---

[31] U.S. Senate, *Hurricane Katrina*, Chapter 26-46.

[32] Louisiana Office of the Governor, "Overview of Governor Kathleen Babineaux Blanco's Actions."

[33] MG Bennett C. Landreneau, Testimony before Homeland Security and Governmental Affairs Committee, U.S. Senate, February 9, 2006. According to General Honoré and General Blum, General Landreneau first asked for troops on August 31. U.S. Senate, *Hurricane Katrina*, Chapter 26-51.

[34] Kathleen Babineaux Blanco, Governor of Louisiana, Testimony before the Committee on Homeland Security and Governmental Affairs, U.S. Senate, February 2, 2006. This was the same day that the TAG asked the NGB to coordinate the National Guard response and the day the decision was made to send two National Guard division headquarters. According to General Honoré and General Blum, General Landreneau first asked for troops on August 31. U.S. Senate, *Hurricane Katrina*, Chapter 26-51.

[35] Louisiana Office of the Governor, "Overview of Governor Kathleen Babineaux Blanco's Actions." According to the Louisiana TAG, the governor did not specify the type of troops (National Guard or active) in the figure 40,000. (U.S. Senate, *Hurricane Katrina*, Chapter 26–59).

[36] DoD, press briefing.

rization is received, conduct crowd control and security in the vicinity of New Orleans."[37]

Responding to warning orders over the next days, the Division Ready Brigade of the 82nd Airborne Division increased the state of readiness of all of its 5,000 soldiers.[38] The Second Brigade Combat Team of the First Cavalry Division prepared for a mission that would likely involve search and rescue, evacuation, debris removal, traffic control, and commodity distribution. The commander of the Second Marine Expeditionary Force also began to make plans to provide not only aircraft and engineering equipment but also air and ground forces. The 24th Marine Expeditionary Unit, an infantry battalion of 1,200 Marines, was postured at the highest state of readiness.[39]

Then, on September 2, Governor Blanco wrote to the president: "Based on our initial assessment, I have previously requested significant federal support to include: an additional 40,000 troops as well as for military vehicles."[40] She met that same day with President Bush and reiterated her request for support from a significant number of federal troops.[41]

The next day, September 3, President Bush ordered the deployment of more than 7,200 Army and Marine land forces to Louisiana.[42] By comparison, the response to Hurricane Andrew in 1992 involved just over 23,800 active-duty service members in addition to over 6,300 National Guard troops.[43] The Army and Marine units deployed to respond to Hurricane Katrina were not selected for any special or

---

[37] U.S. Senate, *Hurricane Katrina*, Chapter 26-30.

[38] U.S. Senate, *Hurricane Katrina*, Chapter 26-31.

[39] U.S. Senate, *Hurricane Katrina*, Chapter 26-32.

[40] Blanco, letter to the president, September 2, 2005.

[41] U.S. Senate, *Hurricane Katrina*, Chapter 26-65. See also, Louisiana Office of the Governor, "Overview of Governor Kathleen Babineaux Blanco's Actions."

[42] The White House, "President Addresses Nation: Discusses Hurricane Katrina Relief Efforts," Washingotn, D.C., September 3, 2005.

[43] See Joint Task Force Andrew (JTF Andrew), "Overview Brief," n.d.

unique capabilities, but rather to carry out humanitarian relief. They were specifically not sent for purposes of law enforcement.[44]

While lead elements from the Army and Marine units arrived in Louisiana the day after the president's decision, most were not on the ground until two days later, and the full deployment was not completed until four days after the president's order to deploy.[45] Although their deployment came after the Superdome and convention center evacuations had been completed, these active-duty forces did undertake house-to-house search and rescue; they also conducted presence patrols to help create a sense of security in the affected Louisiana parishes.[46]

Figure 3.6 shows the types of active-duty Army units that were deployed in Hurricane Andrew in 1992 and Hurricane Floyd in 1999. The National Guard contributed to these responses, but in relatively small numbers. The types of active-duty units deployed in response to the Los Angeles riots in 1992 (along with federalized National Guard units) are also shown. These deployments are then compared with the types of National Guard and active-duty units deployed in response to Hurricane Katrina. The similarity of the types of units deployed in all of these responses is particularly noteworthy.

While it is difficult to find a direct link between the outcome of the federal response effort and the types of military units sent or the exact timing of their arrival in Louisiana or Mississippi, it is clear that the time it took for Army and Marine land forces to deploy contributed to the delays in evacuating the Superdome and the convention center and in accomplishing search and rescue operations across the two states.

Many considerations were involved in how, why, and when the decision was made to deploy these active-duty land forces. The process

---

[44] U.S. Senate, *Hurricane Katrina*, Chapter 26-58.

[45] The time lines for the active duty response to Hurricane Andrew were similar. JTF Andrew was formed on August 28, 1992, and a week later, 16,000 Army and Marine troops were on the ground.

[46] Governor Blanco testified that what she asked for were people to do some difficult missions that they later did, such as help with the search and rescue. She did not want them to do law enforcement, because she had the National Guard. Blanco, Testimony before the Committee on Homeland Security and Governmental Affairs.

**Figure 3.6**
**Types of Army Units Deployed**

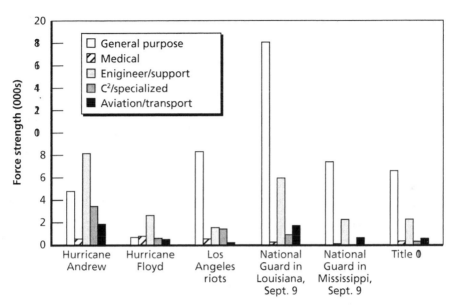

SOURCE: The estimates for the historical cases were derived in 2001 from the U.S. Army Management School Web site, which is no longer accessible. Data on Hurricane Katrina as found in National Guard Bureau GIS Staff, Army National Guard Units in Support of Hurricane Disaster Area, Mississippi and Louisiana, September 9, 2005, and JTF-Katrina daily briefing, September 9, 2005.
RAND *MG603-3.6*

for requesting active-duty forces for local disaster response begins with state officials, because they are in the best position to understand the needs and because DoD's role is to fill gaps in the capabilities of state and other civilian agencies. States forward their requests for assistance to federal civilian officials; the requests then move through a series of military channels (the DCOs, the JTF, and NORTHCOM) to the DoD. There these requests are handled by personnel from both the Office of the Secretary of Defense and the Joint Staff. Requests that are approved are tasked to the appropriate military service and coordinated with Joint Forces Command.[47] Inherent in this process is the need for

---

[47] U.S. Senate, *Hurricane Katrina*, Chapter 26-7; U.S. House, *A Failure of Initiative*, p. 204.

time to assess the capabilities required by each request and to design an appropriate military response.[48]

As this process was just getting under way, the DoD began to recognize the scope of the devastation, and the day after Hurricane Katrina made landfall, the Deputy Secretary of Defense gave the commander of NORTHCOM a "blank check" for "any DoD resources that he believed were reasonably necessary for the Katrina response."[49] Likewise the Chairman of the Joint Chiefs of Staff directed the various services to begin deploying the forces the DoD believed would be needed. As a result, the timing of the decision to deploy active land forces was not a function of delays in requests from the states or FEMA.[50] There were no processes by which needs were matched against specific requirements. Rather the DoD began sending the types of equipment they felt would be required: communications equipment, aerial reconnaissance capabilities, helicopters, transportation equipment, and field hospitals.

The DoD's initial response did not include active-duty Army and Marine land forces. Civilian and military decisionmakers throughout the government apparently judged that the projected flow of National Guard would be sufficient. General Honoré testified that when he arrived in New Orleans on August 31, he did not believe that federal ground forces were needed.[51] According to the Senate report, this view was widely shared within the DoD.[52] The NGB was tracking the flow of guardsmen into Louisiana and Mississippi and providing projec-

---

[48] How effectively this process functioned in Hurricane Katrina is a matter of considerable debate in the "lessons-learned" reports. The White House report finds that the process was slow and bureaucratic and the delays resulted in critical needs not being met (The White House, *Federal Response to Hurricane Katrina*, p. 54). See also U.S. House, *A Failure of Initiative*, p. 205. and U.S. Senate, *Hurricane Katrina*, Executive Summary, pp. 11–12, and Chapter 26.

[49] U.S. Senate, *Hurricane Katrina*, Chapter 26-12; The White House, *The Federal Response to Hurricane Katrina*, p. 42.

[50] U.S. Senate, *Hurricane Katrina*, Chapter 26-12.

[51] LTG Russel Honoré, Commanding General, 1st U.S. Army, Testimony before the Committee on Homeland Security and Governmental Affairs, U.S. Senate, February 9, 2006.

[52] U.S. Senate, *Hurricane Katrina*, Chapter 26-62.

tions. These projections exceeded the actual flow by about 4,000 over the first four days, but by the end of the first week, there were almost 15,000 National Guard personnel in Louisiana.

Another consideration in the timing of the deployment of active-duty Army and Marine forces involved the availability of units, given overseas deployments. The two Marine units sent, the 24th and 11th Marine Expeditionary Units, had pending deployments overseas and were in the middle of predeployment training. There were only a few Army brigades that were not either just back from deployments in Iraq and Afghanistan or about to deploy. The drawback of deploying the few standing-ready brigades to respond to Hurricane Katrina was that the DoD would have to turn to other, less ready units if an unexpected contingency were to arise overseas. In the end, both the "light infantry" and "heavy" Army ready brigades were sent to Louisiana, including the Division Ready Brigade from the 82nd Airborne Division, generally viewed as the Army's most rapidly deployable contingency force.

Civilian and military officials were also hesitant to deploy federal land forces in the deteriorating law-enforcement environment. Reports of violence in New Orleans appeared immediately, and there were concerns about deploying active-duty federal forces to the area given the constraints of Posse Comitatus. According to the Senate report, the flexibility of using the National Guard for law enforcement was a "significant motive" for relying on the National Guard rather than active-duty forces.[53] This was combined with a general reluctance among the DoD and the NGB leadership to turn to active-duty land Army and Marine forces in domestic emergencies.

The time line for the accomplishment of rescue and relief operations after Hurricane Katrina was a function of when active land forces were able to begin operations, which in turn depended on the timing of the decisions to alert and deploy these forces, as well as the time it took to ready and transport the forces. However, even if decisions had been made earlier to alert these forces (on the same day that JTF-Katrina was formed) and deploy these forces (the day after hurricane landfall), and using the same time lines for readying and transporting the units,

---

[53] U.S. Senate, *Hurricane Katrina*, Chapter 26-48.

most of the Army and Marine forces would still not have been available until after the evacuations of the Superdome and convention center were completed.

As in the case of the National Guard, this suggests that the actual time line for the deployment of active-duty forces in response to Hurricane Katrina may be about what the nation can expect in future catastrophic domestic emergencies, given current capabilities and planning assumptions.

## The Command and Control System

The military operations conducted in response to Hurricane Katrina were multifaceted. During the response stage there were three different types of operations: (1) initial search and rescue operations in Louisiana and Mississippi during the week following the storm, conducted largely by helicopters; (2) the evacuation of the convention center and the Superdome in New Orleans, also in the week after the storm, done by ground transport vehicles; and (3) relief operations across Mississippi and Louisiana, including the transport of supplies, clearing of debris, restoration of critical transport and communications networks, and house-to-house search and rescue operations in New Orleans.

The lessons-learned reports focus on many different aspects of these operations, finding, for example, a lack of situational awareness on the part of federal military forces as to what National Guard forces were in the area and how they were operating.[54] Perhaps the biggest problem identified in these reports was the lack of reliable and interoperable communications, which made it extremely difficult for responders to coordinate emergency response operations.[55] The lessons-learned reports attribute many of these problems to deficiencies in the $C^2$ structure and, specifically, to the separation of the command arrangements

---

[54] The White House, *The Federal Response to Hurricane Katrina*, p. 55; U.S. House, *A Failure of Initiative*, p. 224.

[55] The White House, *The Federal Response to Hurricane Katrina*, p. 37; U.S. House, *A Failure of Initiative*, p. 226.

between active-duty and National Guard forces.[56] We examined possible links between the efficacy of $C^2$ structures and the speed and effectiveness of the response.

Many different $C^2$ arrangements were employed in the military response to Hurricane Katrina. The National Guard troops mobilized to state active duty by the governors of Louisiana and Mississippi were under the command of their TAGs. The governors, through the TAGs, also had "tactical control" (TACON) of the National Guard forces that came from other states.[57] These National Guard forces were deployed as distinct (inseparable) units. Because of the substantial number of National Guard forces involved in the response, the Chief of the NGB decided to deploy a National Guard division headquarters to Louisiana and to Mississippi to assist the TAGs in exercising operational control of the out-of-state forces. They, too, were subordinate to the Mississippi or Louisiana TAG.

As the storm passed, search and rescue operations began immediately, initially conducted by the U.S. Coast Guard and then augmented by Air Force, National Guard, Army, Navy, and some civilian helicopters. Over the first week of the response, these helicopters performed over 900 search and rescue, evacuation, and supply delivery missions.[58] No unified $C^2$ system was put in place during these operations—available aircraft spontaneously joined in the efforts to save lives. Many operated under their own tasking orders and relied on their own airspace coordinators.[59] This had the effect of multiple rescue teams operating in the same areas, while other areas were left uncovered. Once successful rescues were made, there was no formal direction on where

---

[56] According to the White House report, the "fragmented deployment system and lack of an integrated command structure for both active duty and National Guard forces exacerbated communications and coordination issues during the initial response," and it also "resulted in confusion over roles and responsibilities between National Guard and federal forces." The White House, *The Federal Response to Hurricane Katrina*, pp. 43, 55.

[57] These forces were technically "on loan" from their state TAG. The White House, *The Federal Response to Hurricane Katrina*, p. 55.

[58] The White House, *The Federal Response to Hurricane Katrina*, p. 43.

[59] U.S. House, *A Failure of Initiative*, pp. 221, 231.

to take those rescued.[60] The House report found that the urgent emphasis on getting victims to high ground meant that evacuees were often stranded at air-evacuation drop-off points, with the result that people saved from flood waters often suffered—some for days—in sweltering conditions, some without food or water.[61]

The overwhelming task of evacuating New Orleans led Governor Blanco to ask JTF-Katrina commander General Honoré, upon his arrival on August 31, to plan and coordinate these efforts.[62] He turned to a 5th Army planning staff sent to support the Louisiana DCO, which coordinated and provided $C^2$ for the air and ground evacuations from the Superdome, the convention center, and the Interstate 10 causeway. The evacuations themselves were carried out by National Guard troops.[63] The coordination between General Honoré and his staffs with the National Guard was informal.

DoD established JTF-Katrina the day after Hurricane Katrina made landfall, and the federal $C^2$ structure was built up over the coming week as active-duty units of the different military services arrived. Initially, operations were coordinated primarily through liaison arrangements using the Emergency Preparedness Liaison Officers.

In asking for significant federal military assistance, Governor Blanco opposed giving up her command of National Guard troops, favoring a separate $C^2$ structure for active-duty forces.[64] Governor Blanco's view was initially shared by senior leaders in Washington,

---

[60] The White House, *The Federal Response to Hurricane Katrina*, p. 57.

[61] U.S. House, *A Failure of Initiative*, p. 231.

[62] According to the Louisiana Office of the Governor, the Governor wanted the Louisiana TAG to be able to focus on saving lives, search and rescue, and law and order. Louisiana Office of the Governor, "Overview of Governor Kathleen Babineaux Blanco's Actions."

[63] U.S. House, A Failure of Initiative, p. 194 includes a FEMA member's claim that the evacuation of the Superdome was delayed for 24 hours by having Honoré take over the evacuation operations. General Honoré disputes this claim. See LTG Russel Honoré, Letter to Select Bipartisan Committee to Investigate the Preparation for and Response to Hurricane Katrina, February 21, 2006.

[64] U.S. Senate, *Hurricane Katrina*, Chapter 26-57-58.

including Secretary of Defense Donald Rumsfeld and General Blum.[65] However, once it became clear that large numbers of active-duty land forces would be deployed to the area, views in Washington changed. On the September 2, senior DoD civilian and military leaders recommended to the president a dual-hat command structure, which the White House in turn presented to Governor Blanco.[66]

After considering and rejecting federalizing the National Guard, President Bush proposed a hybrid approach, whereby General Honoré, as commander of JTF-Katrina, would have been made a member of the Louisiana National Guard and then National Guard troops in state active-duty status in Louisiana would have been put under his command. As a dual-status commander, General Honoré would have served as commander of federal troops under the Secretary of Defense and as commander of the National Guard forces under Governor Blanco.[67]

Governor Blanco rejected the president's proposal, believing that her TAG was successfully overseeing the operations of the National Guard and that the evacuation efforts under the command of General Honoré were complementing the National Guard effort.[68] Thus, National Guard and active-duty units were deployed in Louisiana and Mississippi with separate $C^2$ structures throughout the response to Hurricane Katrina. Units were assigned different geographic areas in which to carry out various relief and rescue missions.[69] There were some reports of active-duty forces moving into areas already being patrolled by National Guard units and of National Guard units being diverted from their missions to transport and support active-duty forces. But for

---

[65] U.S. House, *A Failure of Initiative*, pp. 221, 206. FEMA Director, Michael Brown has stated that he concluded that FEMA, state, and local capabilities were inadequate and favored federalizing the response, i.e., invoking the Insurrection Act and placing the National Guard under the command of active duty forces. U.S. Senate, *Hurricane Katrina*, Chapter 26-56-58.

[66] U.S. Senate, *Hurricane Katrina*, Chapter 26-63-68.

[67] See Kathleen Babineaux Blanco, Governor of Louisiana, Draft Letter to the President of the United States, with attached Memorandum of Agreement, dated September 2, 2005.

[68] Louisiana Office of the Governor, "Overview of Governor Kathleen Babineaux Blanco's Actions."

[69] The White House, *The Federal Response to Hurricane Katrina*, p. 43.

the most part, the units operated independently, and limited coordination was achieved through the state TAGs and JTF-Katrina.

By the end of the first week of the response, the military forces in Mississippi and Louisiana had grown to over 26,000 National Guard forces and almost 10,000 active-duty forces. The $C^2$ structure that emerged was complex and multifaceted, given that coordination arrangements had to be made among states, between civilians and military organizations at both the state and federal levels, and among multiple military organizations and staffs.

NORTHCOM commanded most active-duty forces through JTF-Katrina.[70] JTF-Katrina in turn commanded the majority of its active-duty forces through separate task forces: a logistics task force and one for each of the services. A planning group from the U.S. 5th Army was deployed to Louisiana under JTF-Katrina to assist FEMA and state and local officials in identifying what DoD assistance was needed. It also helped with the coordination of active-duty and National Guard forces and supported Coast Guard Vice Admiral Thad W. Allen when he became the PFO.

Staffs from other military organizations were also sent to assist in the response to Hurricane Katrina, with separate command arrangements. To coordinate the federal military response with civilian authorities, NORTHCOM deployed under its command DCOs to Mississippi and Louisiana as well as its Standing Joint Force Headquarters. U.S. Joint Forces Command (JFCOM) sent a Standing Joint Force Headquarters to support the PFO in the planning and implementation of federal missions. This unit reported back directly to JFCOM, not to NORTHCOM or JTF-Katrina. Figure 3.7 shows the Hurricane Katrina $C^2$ structure, indicating the different types of military command that were exercised by the various commanders, task forces, and staffs as well as the coordination that took place between the National Guard and the various federal forces.[71]

---

[70] This command arrangement is known as operational control (OPCON).

[71] For background on these different types of command arrangements, see Davis et al., *Army Forces for Homeland Security*, pp. 69–72.

**Figure 3.7**
**Hurricane Katrina Command and Control Structure**

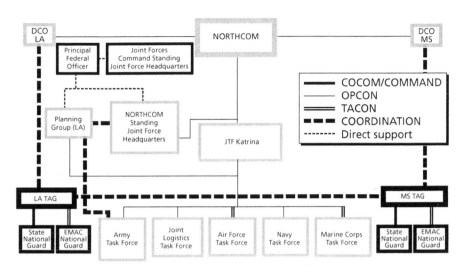

SOURCE: Based on JTF-Katrina Commander's Assessment, September 9, 2005.
RAND *MG603-3.7*

The National Guard and federal C² structures were separate, and the federal C² structure had multiple commanders. That a more unified structure would have made a difference in the outcome of the response is implied in the findings of the lessons-learned reports, although they made no recommendations for change.[72]

Many problems that arose in the military operations conducted in response to Hurricane Katrina were likely due at least in part to deficiencies in the C² structure. Coordination challenges certainly existed between and among the various state and federal chains of command; these challenges were exacerbated initially by poor communications and throughout the response by the difficulty in resolving conflicting

---

[72] U.S. Senate, *Hurricane Katrina*, Chapter 26-68-70, calls for the development of "an integrated plan for the employment of National Guard units" and coordination of DoD support activities with the other federal support activities. But it concludes by saying that "the Committee has not determined that a lack of coordination impaired the effectiveness of the military response to Katrina." It only notes that "many leaders agree that we must establish mechanisms now to ensure unity of effort between the Guard and active duty forces the next time they are called for such a common cause."

needs and desires of state governors and federal military command-ers. In terms of the characteristics of the overall response, however, it is hard to find a direct link between the speed and effectiveness of the response and the multiple and complex $C^2$ structures.

Had an operational and tactical level $C^2$ structure been put in place, and a single person put in charge of the initial search and rescue operations, the evacuations would probably have been accomplished somewhat quicker. There also may have been better coordination between search and rescue teams and the rest of the relief operations in moving those rescued to shelters. The search and rescue operations were limited primarily by the small number of helicopters available relative to the enormous needs. What happened, or did not happen, in the evacuations of the thousands stranded in the Superdome and con-vention center cannot be traced back to the $C^2$ structure, as the main delays in the evacuation process arose as a result of the lack of transpor-tation assets and personnel, including specifically law-enforcement and security personnel. Had a single person been in command of evacua-tion efforts, there might have been ways to introduce National Guard units more quickly into the operations or to speed the arrival of buses or MP units, but the tragedy arising from the slowness of these evacu-ations is unlikely to have been completely avoided.

In the overall relief operations that occurred in Louisiana and Mississippi over the two-week response period, it is also difficult to see how the separate active-duty and reserve $C^2$ structures were a signifi-cant hindrance to operational effectiveness, particularly once the forces were tasked to operate in different geographic regions. The timing and effectiveness of these operations were a function of when the forces arrived rather than how they were commanded. What can be inferred, however, is that the debates at the end of the first week over federal-izing the entire response and over the characteristics of the active-duty and reserve $C^2$ structures were a serious distraction from the business of carrying out actual relief efforts.

## Lessons from Hurricane Katrina

Hurricane Katrina took an enormous toll in terms of deaths, destruction, and human suffering. Our research focused on outlining events as they happened and on uncovering what might have made a difference in the outcome of the response. We discovered that although deficiencies on the civilian side stand out, so do the limitations of the response capability of the military—including both the National Guard and active-duty forces—and what it was able to provide in the immediate aftermath of the hurricane.

Decisionmakers had a good understanding of the magnitude of the destruction and the response capability required. While the multiple and complex $C^2$ structures contributed to some coordination problems, the response was delayed primarily by a lack of civilian and military responders, transportation assets, and relief supplies. The events following Hurricane Katrina suggest that the size and time lines of the military response may be about what the nation can expect following future catastrophic emergencies, given current Army capabilities and planning assumptions. The processes for requesting and approving the flow of National Guard units were short-circuited by the NGB's general call for help, but it still took time to find volunteers, ready the units, transport them to the region, assign them to specific relief efforts in the disaster area, and get them fully operational. Active-duty military forces were immediately involved in the search and rescue operations, but the delay in deciding to alert and deploy active-duty land forces reflected the nation's historical approach to providing federal capabilities to assist with domestic emergencies. While DoD gave NORTHCOM a "blank check" to provide response resources early on, time was needed to assess the needs and potential gaps in civilian and National Guard capabilities. The magnitude of the deficiencies became clear as the first week of the response ended; at that point, the decision to deploy more than 7,000 active-duty land forces was made. However, even if a decision to deploy a large number of active-duty land forces had been made on the day of hurricane landfall, their arrival would still have occurred after the evacuations of the Superdome and convention center were complete. These lessons from Hurricane Katrina led us to consider whether changes are needed in how the Army prepares to respond to catastrophic domestic emergencies with National Guard and active-duty military forces.

# CHAPTER FOUR

# Implications for Army Planning and Operations

After completing a review of the events and time line of the military response to Hurricane Katrina, we turned our attention to the question of whether changes in the roles and responsibilities of the National Guard and active-duty forces during domestic emergencies would enable them to better respond. We also investigated whether new $C^2$ arrangements are needed among the military forces operating within the United States.

## Roles and Responsibilities of National Guard and Active Forces

In responding to domestic emergencies, the United States is likely to continue to give primary responsibility to local and state officials, who best understand the situations as they arise, have the kinds of capabilities that will be needed, and can respond quickly. In addition, the Constitution's delineation of the limits of federal authority generally supports the primacy of the state in responding to disasters, a primacy that extends to both civilian and National Guard responders. However, in extreme catastrophic domestic emergencies, whether they be hurricanes, earthquakes, or terrorist attacks, the response needs may be well beyond those that individual states can provide, and assistance will be required not only from civilians in the federal government but also from active-duty military forces.

Defining any approach to the provision of such support must take account of both the nation's historical preference for a local and civilian response and the reality of the potential needs that can arise after a catastrophe. The lessons of Hurricane Katrina call for us to look for ways to achieve a quicker and more robust federal response and to identify any changes needed in the responsibilities of the National Guard and active-duty Army in preparing for and responding to major domestic emergencies.

## Army Transformation

The U.S. Army is transforming in many different ways to meet the challenges facing the nation, both at home and abroad. Both active-duty and National Guard forces are transforming to smaller modular and interoperable combat and support brigades that provide the foundation for an expeditionary force capable of quickly providing units tailored to a specific threat. The Army is expanding its active-duty combat force, and National Guard forces are restructuring into a smaller number of lighter combat brigades. Both are transforming to make all their brigades more flexible. The Army is also rebalancing the types of units making up its active-duty force so as to reduce the stress on some of its forces.[1]

In addition, the Army is implementing the Army Force Generation (ARFORGEN) process, whereby units move through a structured and predictable process of unit readiness over time, resulting in recurring periods of availability for missions at home and overseas. Units in the active-duty Army, the USAR, and the National Guard will flow through force pools, designated as Reset/Train, Ready, and Available (see Figure 4.1). All of these units could be called upon in a major domestic emergency, though they will be in different states of training and have different levels of equipment.

The Army's goal is for active-duty units to be on a three-year cycle, with one deployment in three years. For reserve units, the cycle is planned for five to six years, with one deployment in each cycle. Given the current high level of overseas requirements, the Army recognizes that it will be a number of years before these goals can be met. The

---

[1]  For a description of these plans, see U.S. Army, *2006 Posture Statement,* February 10, 2006.

**Figure 4.1**
**Army ARFORGEN Process**

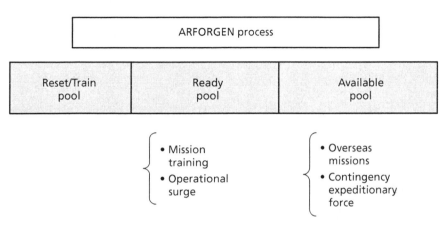

RAND *MG603-4.1*

duration and activities in each of the force pools may vary by unit or mission. Those in the Ready pool continue training in preparation for their assigned mission, but they are available to meet operational surge requirements and, in the case of the National Guard, can be mobilized if needed. Units are planned to remain in the Available pool for one year at a time. Some in this pool will be deployed on missions overseas, and others will be in a contingency expeditionary force.[2] State governors will have approximately 50 percent of their National Guard forces available for use at all times. Approximately 25 percent will be involved in intensive training and preparation for deployment, and the remaining 25 percent to be deployed overseas or in a contingency expeditionary force. National Guard units would be mobilized and deployed for periods of time ranging from 9 to 18 months.[3]

## National Guard

The roles and responsibilities of the National Guard are expanding at home and overseas. While they remain critical to governors for

---

[2] See U.S. Army, *Army Campaign Plan*, Annex F (ARFORGEN Implementation Plan) to Army Campaign Plan Change 4, July 27, 2006.

[3] See U.S. Army, *Army Campaign Plan: National Guard*. briefing, n.d.

responding to state emergencies, today National Guard units are also engaged in operations to counter the flow of drugs and illegal immigrants into the United States. They are also providing security around key buildings in our nation's capital and elsewhere. Most important, the National Guard is no longer viewed as a strategic reserve, to be mobilized over many months to respond in the event of large conventional wars. Rather, the National Guard is now being used as an operational reserve; guard units are regularly mobilized to participate in operations around the world, including operations currently in progress in Iraq and Afghanistan.

A number of transformation initiatives are under way in the National Guard as a result of 9/11 and Hurricane Katrina. At the initiative of the Congress and in preparation for responding to terrorist attacks involving weapons of mass destruction, the National Guard has nearly completed the creation of 55 WMD-CSTs with the capability to deploy quickly to assist in the detection of and response to the presence of chemical, biological, or nuclear materials. These teams use a sophisticated communications infrastructure capable of connecting many disparate communications systems; they are capable of coordinating the nation's overall response to a catastrophic event. The National Guard, with congressional funding, is also creating Chemical, Biological, Radiological/Nuclear, and Explosive (CBRNE)–Enhanced Response Force Packages (CERFP) Teams with the capability to quickly carry out mass casualty decontamination, medical treatment, security, and urban search and rescue.[4]

States are in the process of setting up Joint Force Headquarters with the capability to assume joint command of state National Guard units from all services, as well as any units that may flow in from other states in an emergency. The White House report called upon the DoD to "consider fully resourcing the JTF State Headquarters" as "key" to the rapid deployment of National Guard forces.[5] States are designating certain units as National Guard Reaction Forces; these units will pro-

---

[4]   While the WMD-CSTs are dedicated to responding to events in the United States, the CERFP Teams are available for use overseas as well as at home.

[5]   The White House, *The Federal Response to Hurricane Katrina*, p. 95.

vide site security, establish check points, and control civil disturbances. According to General Blum, these units are being trained to "respond anywhere in the state with an initial 75- to 125-person element within a minimum of four to eight hours."[6] The NGB has called for ten essential National Guard capabilities needed in each state beyond a Joint Force Headquarters; these include engineering, civil support, security, medical transportation, maintenance, logistics, aviation, and communications. The National Guard has started to dedicate a number of annual training hours to preparing for HLS activities. The NGB is also engaged with NORTHCOM in many initiatives to improve communications among the various civilian organizations and military services.[7]

### Department of Defense Post–Hurricane Katrina Initiatives

The DoD has assigned a DCO to each of the ten DHS/FEMA regional offices; each of these DCOs will have a five member Defense Coordinating Element complement. Both the DCOs and their Defense Coordinating Element will be able to deploy in support of an interagency Joint Field Office, a facility designed to integrate federal, state, local, and private-sector incident management organizations. NORTH-COM has revised its Contingency Plan 2501 for DSCA and is developing a reconnaissance annex that will provide the mechanisms for DoD damage assessment activities. There have also been a number of exercises that have included participation from across the DoD.[8]

JFCOM identified approximately 25,000 troops that the Defense Department could tap to aid other government agencies in hurricane

---

[6]   LTG H. Steven Blum, Chief, National Guard Bureau, Testimony Before the Committee on Armed Services, Subcommittee on Terrorism, Unconventional Threats and Capabilities, House of Representatives, Second Session, 109th Congress, May 25, 2006.

[7]   For a description of these and other National Guard initiatives, see LTG H. Steven, Chief, National Guard Bureau, Statement Before Commission on National Guard and Reserves, May 3, 2006, and Blum, Testimony Before the Committee on Armed Services.

[8]   For these and other DoD and NORTHCOM initiatives in anticipation of the 2006 hurricane season, see Paul McHale, Assistant Secretary of Defense for homeland Defense, Testimony Before the Committee on Armed Services, Subcommittee on Terrorism, Unconventional Threats and Capabilities, House of Representatives, May 25, 2006.

response operations during the 2006 severe storm season. According to press reports, this plan involved four force packages that could be put on a week long "prepare to deploy order," meaning that they could be sent out on very short notice. The first focused on the immediate needs of $C^2$, damage assessment, search and rescue, and communications. The second included "significant" DoD capabilities, including a brigade team, aviation assets for search and rescue, and other medical specialists and engineers. The other two force packages were designed to sustain DoD activities in a disaster area and were geared up for recovery efforts, including those involving mass casualties. Responsibility for funding any operations resided with NORTHCOM.[9] This response was tailored for severe natural disasters, though many of the same types of capabilities would be required during other types of catastrophic domestic emergencies. Although defining and designating these forces packages is an important step toward a quicker federal response capability, the response time lines would still be a function of when the decision to alert and move them is made. The forces actually on alert at any given time would have been similar to those available at the time of Hurricane Katrina.

## Should States Do More?

The question arises as to whether states should, in addition to the initiatives outlined above, make more fundamental changes in their overall approach to responding to catastrophic domestic emergencies.

Rather than having a small number rapid-reaction units in each state, one step would be to ensure, in planning and through exercises, that every National Guard unit is capable of rapid deployment to emergencies not only within their state but also to other states. Plans could also be made by states, through arrangements within their EMAC agreements, to ensure that out-of-state National Guard units are prepared to fill in for state units that are mobilized and deployed over-

---

[9]  A description of these force packages can be found in Sebastian Sprenger, *Inside the Pentagon*, August 31, 2006.

seas. Such standing agreements would enhance the quickness of the response of units from neighboring states.

Another step would be for governors to design and implement plans designating certain of their state units with different types of capabilities for HLS out-of-state responses; in the event of a major domestic emergency, governors would be prepared to call these units involuntarily to state active duty, in the same way that governors call up units when emergencies occur within their own states. Guardsmen in these units would supplement those expected to volunteer and could be given some additional training in HLS operations, including participating in exercises with civilian first responders.

State governors, along with the NGB, could create plans for using the Air National Guard to transport predesignated units to out-of-state emergencies. Alternatively, or in addition, arrangements could be made to employ the federal Civil Reserve Air Fleet (CRAF) for transporting these state units using commercial airlines.[10]

Finally, to help states become better prepared for HLS emergencies, the DoD could assign the National Guard of each state a specific federal mission to be prepared to conduct HLS activities both within the state and in other states requesting assistance. This would permit National Guard units to receive Title 32 funding from DoD for HLS training and for the conduct of preplanned HLS activities (such as exercises) with units from other states or civilian organizations, similar to how counterdrug operations are conducted today.[11]

---

[10] The CRAF is made up of aircraft and personnel provided by U.S. civilian air carriers under contract with DoD. The program is designed to provide certain numbers and kinds of aircraft quickly in the event of different levels of DoD requirements at home and abroad. U.S. Air Force, "Civil Reserve Air Fleet," fact sheet, January 2007.

[11] For a more detailed description of characteristics of this option, including training, personnel, legal issues, and command and control, see Davis et al., *Army Forces for Homeland Security*, pp. 18–22.

## Should There Be a Regional Approach?

Most post–Hurricane Katrina National Guard transformation initia-tives are largely focused on preparations by and among individual states. The question arises as to whether there is a need for additional prepa-rations with a regional-level focus, preparation that could be made in conjunction with the regional-level efforts of FEMA and other civilian organizations.[12] These steps could build upon state-to-state compacts that now exist in some regions.

The annex to the *Army Campaign Plan* that outlines the steps for implementing the ARFORGEN process in the National Guard recognizes the "need to mitigate shortfalls and respond to regional DSCA requirements."[13] But it does not lay out in any detail what this might call for in terms of planning and equipping within the National Guard.

An earlier RAND analysis, *Army Forces for Homeland Security*, called for the design of a multifaceted hedging strategy for facing future homeland security risks; this strategy focused on a regional approach to the use of the National Guard. It called for the creation of standing regional homeland security task forces across the country, with units dedicated to and trained for HLS and capable of rapid response. The authors illustrated how this might be accomplished through the cre-ation of a new civil support battalion (CSB) in multistate regions—the ten FEMA regions.[14]

Each CSB would be ready to deploy in domestic emergencies within 18 hours of notification. It would be dedicated to responding to domestic emergencies and not available for deployment overseas. The CSBs would be able to carry out all the general HLS tasks, includ-

---

[12] The White House, *The Federal Response to Hurricane Katrina*, pp. 89–91, focuses on put-ting in place a "regional structure for preparedness" in its recommendations for the federal civilian response, but it does not extend this in its recommendations for the military, which are focused on state preparations.

[13] U.S. Army, *Army Campaign Plan*, Annex F, p. F-4-C-7.

[14] For a more detailed description of characteristics of these regional homeland security task forces, including the training, personnel, legal issues, and command and control, see Davis et al., *Army Forces for Homeland Security*, pp. 31–37.

ing communications, emergency medical care, search and rescue, engineering support, and emergency provision of food, water, and shelter. They would also have the ability to support local law enforcement by conducting general security operations.

The CSBs would provide the command and control for augmentation by other National Guard forces from within the state, by CSBs from other regions, or by National Guard units from other states. They would plan and train with civilian local first responders, state and federal civilian agencies, state Joint Force Headquarters, as well as specialized counterterrorism and WMD units.

Each battalion would have approximately 900 soldiers—one-third would be full-time positions, staffed by both National Guard volunteers in Title 32 status and civilian technicians working for the National Guard.[15] The remaining two-thirds would be part-time, drilling guardsmen who agree to be on special ready status so that the governor could call them up within 12 hours. Our CSB force structure was derived from an existing National Guard organization, the Forward Support Battalion, augmented with a communications platoon as well as military police, engineer, and transportation companies. No new National Guard personnel are envisioned in this approach (see Table 4.1).

Each CSB's headquarters detachment would be designed to control other National Guard units from the affected state or region and to accommodate an Air National Guard planning and liaison cell to enhance the CSB with Air National Guard aviation, aeromedical, engineering, and other capabilities. The CSB elements would be under the command of the adjutant general in the state in which they are based, but when deployed to another state, operational control of the CSB would be given to the adjutant general of the receiving state. In the ARFORGEN process, these CSBs would be designated as part of the Theater Committed Structure, which is defined as "deployable," but

---

[15] The Active Guard and Reserve (AGR) comprises personnel on voluntary active duty providing full-time support to Army organizations for the purpose of organizing, administering, or training the Reserve components. No new AGR positions are involved in this approach.

**Table 4.1**
**Illustrative CSB Force Structure**

| Unit Type | Strength |
|---|---|
| Headquarters detachment | 51 |
| Communications platoon | 25 |
| Supply company | 62 |
| Maintenance company | 167 |
| Medical company | 100 |
| Military police company | 177 |
| Transportation company | 167 |
| Engineer company | 145 |
| Total | 894 |

SOURCE: Davis et al., *Army Forces for Homeland Security*, Table 3.3, p. 34.

they would be primarily for use in assigned theaters, which in this case would be the United States. Some of the force structure freed up by Army plans to reduce the number of National Guard combat brigades could be used to create the CSBs.

Had CSBs been available at the time of Hurricane Katrina, one could have deployed to Mississippi and one to Louisiana within hours of hurricane landfall, or possibly even in advance. Their communications package could have supplemented that available in the state emergency headquarters, and they could have immediately begun planning relief operations—including evacuations—and helped direct the flow of National Guard units from other states to the areas where they were needed most. Many of the units arriving would have already been familiar with the CSB from planning activities and exercises. The CSBs could also have helped assess the requirements for different types of units and made it possible for the out-of-state governors and the NGB to send those most needed. The CSB would have reduced the need for the WMD-CSTs' communications capabilities and, thus, not required their diversion from their focus on being ready for a WMD attack. While a division headquarters might still have been needed in Louisiana, it is possible that the CSB could have handled the $C^2$ needs in Mississippi. At a minimum, the CSBs could have filled the initial gap in the states' and National Guard's communications and planning capabilities.

The Center for Strategic and International Studies (CSIS) has recommended a similar approach, calling for ten regional Civil Support Forces that would be "responsible for regional planning, training, and exercising and would be able to deploy initial response forces rapidly to the scene of an event."[16] In their approach, the Civil Support Forces would be dedicated to HLS operations, able to deploy within 12 to 24 hours, and include units with capabilities like those of our CSB. The approaches differ in that the CSIS approach draws on state joint force headquarters and National Guard combat service and combat service support units, while our approach would create a new and dedicated task force and civil support force structure. The CSIS report also goes into greater detail in describing the types of training and exercises that these forces would undertake, from where in the ARFORGEN cycle the Civil Support Force units would be drawn, and the need for pre-identified airlift capabilities to ensure that the time lines for the deployments are achieved.[17]

As part of a regional response, another possibility would be to assign each National Guard division the responsibility to plan for employment as an operational headquarters for HLS missions. The division could be assigned one or more of the civil support forces (i.e., the CSBs described above), for which it would have a habitual relationship for training, exercises, and operational employment. When a division is alerted of an upcoming overseas operational deployment, its HLS responsibilities would be assigned to one of the remaining National Guard divisions. Along with this transfer of responsibility would come the special relationship with the specific civil support forces. Having a division headquarters identified to be the higher headquarters of a

---

[16]  Christine E. Wormuth, Michele A. Flournoy, Patrick T. Henry, Clark A. Murdock, *The Future of the National Guard and Reserves*, Washington, D.C.: CSIS, July 2006., p. 74.

[17]  Wormuth et al., *The Future of the National Guard and Reserves*, pp. 74–78.

specified civil support force during a catastrophic emergency would enable that force to deploy rapidly into a disaster zone during the initial phase of a crisis response while being supported by—eventually subsumed by—the more robust division headquarters if the disaster so warranted, which. This structure would enable the division's significant $C^2$ capabilities to move seamlessly into and out of an affected state whenever needed.

## Should National Guard or Active-Duty Forces in ARFORGEN Be Designated for HLS?

Even if these steps were undertaken, the number of National Guard forces they cover would be fairly small by comparison to the potential magnitude and urgency of the needs arising from a future catastrophic domestic emergency. Moreover, the percentage of National Guard units available to state governors under ARFORGEN is estimated to be less than what was available on average in the states at the time of Hurricane Katrina.

The ARFORGEN process offers possibilities for doing more. There is flexibility in the ARFORGEN process to tailor the timing of National Guard unit mobilizations and to determine training to be done in advance of mobilization. All units will also spend some time training after mobilization. One possibility is that in addition to the current minimal HLS training that National Guard units receive, each National Guard unit in the Ready pool would pursue some additional HLS training activities, such as exercising with civilian first responders and preparing to deploy quickly to emergencies both within and outside their state. This could be done pre- or post-mobilization, depending upon the missions planned for the unit. In this way, National Guard units in the Ready and Available pools would be better prepared if circumstances were to arise that required them quickly to respond to a domestic emergency.

An additional possibility is for some National Guard units in the ARFORGEN process to be given HLS as their primary mission, with their training and readiness tailored accordingly. So rather than preparing to deploy overseas or having a contingency overseas mission, these units would be available to the nation for domestic emergencies once they moved into the Available pool. They would be designated under the ARFORGEN process as Theater Committed (i.e., deployable), but primarily intended for deployment within the United States. As they would be mobilized under Title 10, they would operate under the constraints of Posse Comitatus. Another way to achieve the same goal would be to designate National Guard units for HLS in the Available pool, but have them remain on state active-duty status (instead of mobilizing them to active duty) and have their operations funded under Title 32—as is currently the case in counterdrug operations. This would avoid constraints on the ability of these units to undertake law-enforcement operations.

While the National Guard response to Hurricane Katrina depended upon volunteers without any special HLS training or preparations, under the model outlined above, one or more of the National Guard units in the ARFORGEN Available pool would be trained for HLS emergency operations and ready to respond very quickly. The size of a future response would then become a function of how many in these pools were actually designated in advance or chosen to respond at the time.

At any one time in the ARFORGEN process, only a few National Guard combat and support brigades will be in the Ready and Available pools. A far larger number of active-duty and USAR units are in these pools, and they have capabilities for HLS similar to those in the National Guard. Some would even argue that the types of units in the USAR are better-suited for such responses. Not many USAR units were used in Hurricane Katrina, given the current overseas demands on their capabilities and the statutory limitations on their use in domestic emergencies.

Another possibility for achieving a quick and robust response to catastrophic emergencies would be to turn more quickly to active-duty Army units. All active-duty units in the United States are viewed by FORSCOM and NORTHCOM as available to respond to domestic emergencies up until a few months before their deployment overseas. But as they move through the Ready pool and into the Available pool, their primary focus in preparation and training is for their upcoming overseas mission. Certain active combat and support brigades in the Available pool could be selected for domestic emergency response missions instead of overseas contingencies. These units would take steps to be able to react very quickly if called upon in a domestic emergency, tailoring in advance their equipment and transportation assets to such a contingency. Although Theater Committed under the ARFORGEN process and planned primarily for use in the United States, they could still be deployed overseas if necessary.

Each of these possibilities provides for active-duty units that could act as a reserve force for responding to catastrophic domestic emergencies, alleviating the need to rely on the overseas "ready brigades," as happened in Hurricane Katrina.

## Command and Control Structure

While it is difficult to find a direct link between the multiple and complex military $C^2$ structures in Hurricane Katrina and the speed and effectiveness of the response, no one disputes that there were coordination problems. Given the potential need for large numbers of military forces in catastrophic domestic emergencies, we asked whether new $C^2$ arrangements need to be designed for the military forces operating within the United States.

The $C^2$ structure used in Hurricane Katrina reflected both current military planning and how the military had historically conducted domestic emergency response. As forces arrived during the initial response phase, National Guard and active-duty forces operated independently of one another; over time they began to coordinate their efforts through liaison arrangements. With the creation of JTF-Katrina, these liaison arrangements became more formalized.

As the number of forces responding to Hurricane Katrina grew, the question arose as to whether to move to a more unified $C^2$ structure for National Guard and active-duty units. This issue was debated both within the federal government and by federal officials and the governor of Louisiana for more than 24 hours before a structure of separate active-duty and National Guard task forces was agreed upon; this agreement was not reached until five days after hurricane landfall. Taking time to tailor the $C^2$ structure to the situation is consistent with the view that, because domestic emergencies are different, the $C^2$ structure for each needs to evolve to suit the numbers and types of active-duty, reserve, and National Guard forces called upon to respond.

In responses to small emergencies, this evolution of an overall $C^2$ structure from that which the individual units bring with them to some level of higher coordination or control may be appropriate, as the number of forces and different units responding can be managed through ad hoc $C^2$ arrangements provided their operations are constrained to a limited geographic area. Nevertheless, a catastrophic domestic emergency, especially one occurring without warning, will call for a quick, varied, and robust response from all levels of government; both civilian and military organizations must quickly move to minimize the loss of life and property, especially during the critical first days of the response. Moreover, as the number and diversity of military units involved in a response increase, the ability to coordinate among units to promote a unity of effort becomes more challenging. This suggests that a different approach to defining the military $C^2$ structure may be needed.

One possibility would be to craft a predetermined $C^2$ structure for catastrophic emergencies. This solution has many attractions. It would provide an opportunity for military organizations to conduct exercises using the structure. It would also prevent $C^2$ issues from distracting decisionmakers from the more critical tasks of designing and implementing an effective response. However, the problem with this approach is that we know that there is, in fact, no single $C^2$ structure that would be appropriate for every domestic emergency, as not only will relief needs vary but also the response capabilities of individual states where the disaster hits. There is almost always a need to tradeoff between achieving efficiency through unity of command and addressing the complexity or practicality of the situation through multiple command arrangements. There is also no consensus in the United States today on what single $C^2$ structure should be chosen, as state governors and federal officials have different perspectives on the importance of state sovereignty and, therefore, state control.[18]

Given these facts, we decided to explore an approach that would prepare decisionmakers to decide as quickly as possible on a $C^2$ structure either upon warning or soon after an emergency arose. Because there is no consensus on what $C^2$ structure to choose for any given response operation, there will always be debate among decisionmakers. However, the debate can be limited and shaped by crafting a finite set of alternative $C^2$ structures and clearly outlining the applicability of each to different types of potential emergencies.

In the response to Hurricane Katrina (and in other historical federal disaster responses), the main point of contention over the $C^2$ structure was the relationship between federal and state governments and their control of active-duty and National Guard forces. We began by defining alternative $C^2$ structures that range from those with a significant level of federal control to those with predominantly state control.[19] We excluded an alternative in which the president would federalize the National Guard, as was done in the response to the Los Angeles riots in 1992. In this alternative, all military forces would operate under Title 10 authorities and would be placed under the command of an active-duty commander. The problem with such an alternative is that National Guard forces would be constrained to operating under

---

[18] The case for waiting to determine a $C^2$ structure, and the underlying differences of perspective, can be found in the response by the Secretaries of Homeland Security and Defense to The White House, *The Federal Response to Hurricane Katrina*, p. 94, that called upon DoD and DHS to "develop recommendations for revision of the NRP to delineate the circumstances, objectives, and limitations of when DOD might temporarily assume the lead for the Federal response to a catastrophic incident." They recommended that such a decision be based "on an assessment of the distinctive facts and circumstances of each catastrophic incident" and then went on to define a series of questions that would need to be answered at the time, what they call the "key facts and circumstances." See U.S. Department of Homeland Security, Joint Letter to the President of the United States from Secretary Chertoff and Secretary Rumsfeld, April 7, 2006..

[19] A separate issue is how to define a $C^2$ structure for initial searcha and rescue operations. We have not included this issue in our discussion but would encourage the U.S. government to review the National Search and Rescue Plan in light of the revisions to the NRP and then to not only develop detailed planning but also a $C^2$ structure with a single person in command.

the authorities of the Posse Comitatus Act, unless the Insurrection Act is invoked. While this alternative was considered in response to Hurricane Katrina, it was rejected as there was no cause to invoke the Insurrection Act. We also excluded an alternative that would give the lead entirely to a state. While this is generally what happened in the response to the World Trade Center bombings in New York City, it is unlikely that there would be no need for active-duty forces in future catastrophic emergency responses and, therefore, the need for a federal $C^2$ structure.

Each of the four alternatives presented below includes a mix of active-duty and National Guard forces. All of these alternatives assume the creation of one federal task force and two state task forces. The actual number of state and federal task forces created for any given contingency would be a function of the characteristics of the disaster.

## Alternative 1: Separate Federal and State Task Forces

The first alternative envisions two separate and distinct federal and state military $C^2$ structures (see Figure 4.2). In this alternative, NORTHCOM's JTF would exercise operational control of all Title 10 forces in the area.[20] State National Guard forces would remain under the command of their TAG, and the TAG would exercise operational control of National Guard forces sourced from assisting states under the EMAC. NORTHCOM's subordinate JTF would coordinate (i.e., would have direct liaison authority) with the state joint force headquarters (JFHQ) during the conduct of the operations when the boundaries of their respective designated operating areas overlap or are adjacent. The governor(s) of the affected state(s) would communicate needs both formally through established channels and informally through military coordination channels between NORTHCOM's JTF and the state JFHQ. The approval authority for the employment of federal forces and capabilities would remain within the federal chain of command. This alternative is similar to the $C^2$ structure that emerged during the

---

[20] This JTF could be NORTHCOM's Joint Task Force—Civil Support, Standing Joint Force Headquarters-North (SJFHQ-N), or a JTF created for the specific emergency, as was the case in Hurricane Katrina.

**Figure 4.2**
**Separate Federal and State Task Forces**

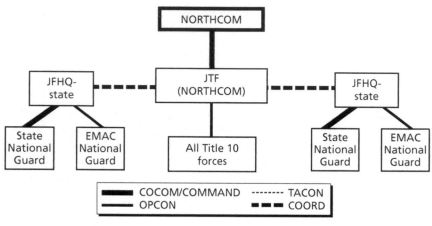

RAND *MG603-4.2*

response to Hurricane Katrina, where the two types of forces mostly operated independently under their own control and were separated into geographic areas of operations.

## Alternative 2: Dual-Status Command

Under this alternative a single individual would be placed in command and assume "tactical control" (TACON) of both Title 10 and National Guard forces. President Bush proposed this $C^2$ structure to Governor Blanco during the Hurricane Katrina response, but she rejected it. In this $C^2$ alternative, the commander would serve as commander of federal troops under the authority of the Secretary of Defense and as commander of both the affected state's and EMAC National Guard forces under the authority of the affected state's governor. Because of a recent revision in public law, a commander activated to Title 10 status may now also maintain Title 32 and state active-duty command authorities, provided the president and appropriate governor agree. In Figure 4.3, we show the NORTHCOM JTF commander in the lead. Alternatively, the state JFHQ could assume tactical control of all units in the response,

**Figure 4.3**
**Dual-Status Command**

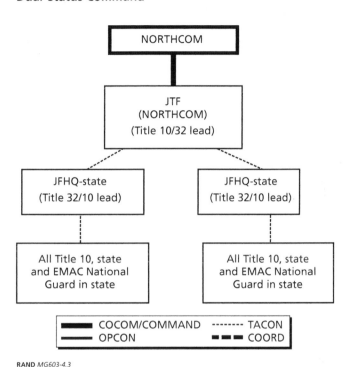

and of active-duty and National Guard forces.[21] The state JFHQ would act as a subordinate C² headquarters for NORTHCOM.[22]

---

[21] In Public Law 108-136, the Congress revised authorities for Title 32 and state active-duty National Guard commanders. In addition, the Secretary has approved new command relationships for operations by Total Force JTFs. The JTFs may now be commanded by National Guard officers in Title 32 or state active-duty status, with an executive officer in Title 10 status to carry out Title 10 authorities. This law specifically applies to National Guard officers—enabling them to exercise control of federal forces. While the statute does not explicitly indicate that a federal officer could be sworn in as a member of a state National Guard and then exercise dual status authority, there is nothing in the language or history of the law to indicate that this was contrary to the intent of Congress. The issue would be whether or not state laws would prevent a federal officer from being temporarily sworn in as a member of its National Guard.

[22] LTG H. Steven Blum, in his Statement Before the Commission on National Guard and Reserves Statement, describes how this might work; he states that the "effectiveness of dual-

## Alternative 3: State Joint Force Headquarters in Lead

Alternative three involves a $C^2$ structure under which NORTHCOM would exercise operational control of the Title 10 forces through its subordinate JTF, as in the first alternative. The command arrangements for the National Guard would also be the same as in the first alternative. Yet unlike the first alternative, under this alternative NORTHCOM would place the Title 10 forces under the tactical control of the state JFHQ to carry out the response operations. While under tactical control of the affected state(s), federal forces could "take orders" from the state military chain of command consistent with existing federal orders, regulations, and policies. Thus, while the formal federal chain of command, which by statute requires an unbroken line between the president and the individual soldier, sailor, airman, or marine, would remain inviolate, tasking authority for certain agreed-upon missions would be granted to the state.[23] Figure 4.4 provides a graphical representation of this alternative.

## Alternative 4: NORTHCOM in Lead

Alternative four would have NORTHCOM exercise operational control of the Title 10 forces through its subordinate JTF. The TAG would exercise command of the state National Guard forces and operational control of National Guard forces from other states. Then, the NORTHCOM subordinate JTF would assume tactical control of all

---

hatted command was proven in 2004 at the G8 Summit, Operation Winter Freeze, as well as the Democratic and Republican National Conventions."

[23] Under this alternative, if a federal officer believes that he is being asked to do something inconsistent with federal guidelines and authorities, he or she would be free to delay acting upon such requests until the issue was resolved through the federal chain of command. When U.S. forces conduct multilateral operations that are led by foreign commanders, they are placed under the operational control of that commander. This issue was examined thoroughly in 1993 during the drafting of Presidential Decision Directive 25, Reforming Multilateral Peacekeeping Operations. During this deliberative process, each of the services, the joint staff, and the Office of the Secretary of Defense agreed that this type of arrangement preserved the federal chain of command and, therefore, was not a violation of existing federal statutes or military practices. Using the logic and rationale employed in PDD-25, there is no legal reason why federal forces could not be temporarily placed under the tactical control of individual states for a specific time, place, and mission.

**Figure 4.4**
**State Joint Force Headquarters in Lead**

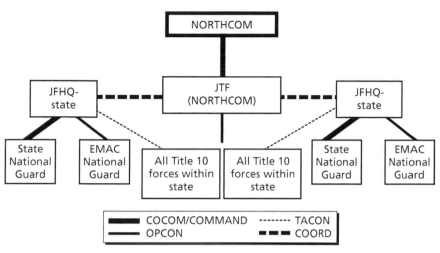

the National Guard forces operating in the state (see Figure 4.5). As in alternative two, although the state would retain command of its forces, it would temporarily relinquish tactical control for a specific time, place, and mission. In this alternative, the federal military chain of command would have limited authority to give tasking orders to designated elements of the National Guard—as long as such orders were consistent with state orders, regulations, and policies. The National Guard forces would not be federalized and so would not operate under the constraints of Posse Comitatus. The NORTHCOM JTF commander would need to be cognizant of this fact, employing the National Guard in law-enforcement situations and the Title 10 forces in non–law enforcement situations.

## Matching the C² Structure to Disaster Response Characteristics

This approach to C² begins by defining the likely range of alternatives from which decisionmakers would choose depending on the characteristics of the emergency, with a particular focus on catastrophic emergencies that require a significant federal military response. The four

**Figure 4.5**
**NORTHCOM in Lead**

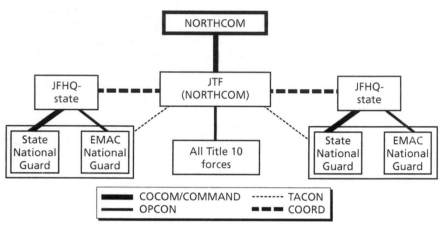

RAND *MG603-4.5*

alternatives outlined above are a good place to begin this process. And, while all disasters are different, some of the characteristics of various types can be defined in advance. The types of military units that are likely to be called upon in a response can also be estimated based on existing capabilities and historical experiences.

The next step in this approach would be to understand how potential disaster characteristics relate to $C^2$ structures that place more or less control at the federal or state level, recognizing that the characteristics are unlikely to all point in the same direction. Even after completing such an analysis, decisionmakers are unlikely to agree on a single $C^2$ structure for a given emergency type immediately. However, such an analysis would provide a basis for an efficient debate and decisionmaking process—particularly if $C^2$ alternatives and disaster characteristics are understood and discussed (and possibly exercised) in advance of events.

**Size.** In accordance with the underlying philosophy of the NRP and the nation's historical preference for relying on local and state resources to respond to catastrophic disasters, as the size of a disaster increases, the role of the federal government and military forces increases. For example, as the number of states involved or the number of terrorist incidents increases, the case for a $C^2$ structure with a federal lead becomes stronger. It is not possible to say at what point alternatives stressing federal control should be chosen over those stressing state control, because the capabilities needed to respond effectively and the need for federal assistance will differ from state to state, and also within areas of states. Therefore, it will be necessary to consider the availability and capabilities of state resources, including those of civilian agencies, the affected state's National Guard, and any National Guard resources available through EMAC, when defining the $C^2$ structure. Similarly, as the number of states affected increases, the potential contribution from out-of-state EMAC forces may decrease, with a resulting increase in the need for federal assistance.

**Warning.** Advanced warning of a catastrophe could, depending on what steps are taken in response to it, either reduce or increase the case for a greater federal lead. If the response to such warning is robust and timely at the federal level, then the case for a federal lead could increase, as there will be time for federal military units to plan and preposition assets. But if such a response is successful in enhancing the capabilities of the affected states (for example, by prepositioning relief supplies), it could make it possible for the state to implement the response with less federal assistance than might otherwise be required. There would then be a case for a state lead in $C^2$.

In the event of no warning, a federal lead may be called upon in the face of a state or states being overwhelmed, but depending on the nature of the emergency, the state in the lead may have the only immediately available response capability, as in an earthquake or a terrorist attack.

Warning is not, however, a binary characteristic; that is, there may be some uncertainty about warning for some disasters, particularly in the case of potential terrorist attacks. An elevated threat level caused by specific intelligence, for example, may constitute some degree of warning. Planning may also serve as a proxy for warning in some cases. While earthquakes occur without warning, response planning in earthquake-prone areas could result in the preestablishment of some joint $C^2$ structures and coordination.

**Emergency Type.** The type of emergency is also an important characteristic in defining a military $C^2$ system. In a terrorist attack, the need to respond in law-enforcement/investigative capacity enhances the case for a federal lead, as does the expected need for the president to demonstrate political resolve. This case would be even stronger were there to be multiple terrorist attacks across more than one state. A federal lead could also be called for in types of disasters that would initially resemble terrorist attacks, such as an explosion of a large chemical storage facility or an unexplained disease outbreak. On the other hand, well-prepared states may be able to successfully accomplish a response in these cases, thereby calling for a state $C^2$ lead. A state lead could also be attractive to the president if he wanted to hold federal assets in reserve for the possibility of subsequent terrorist attacks.

**Availability of Military Forces.** Catastrophic domestic emergencies will likely involve both active-duty and National Guard forces. However, their availability will depend on other state and DoD commitments. Apart from recurring demands for overseas deployments, the number of active-duty forces available to respond to HLS emergencies is a function of the need to have them available for unforeseen overseas contingencies or postured for homeland defense. If few active-duty forces are available or chosen for the response, the case for a federal lead will be reduced.

## Choosing a $C^2$ Structure

It is clear that these disaster characteristics are related in many ways. An appropriate $C^2$ structure cannot be chosen based on any one characteristic alone, and the characteristics will have to be weighted differently for different disasters. However, consideration of these characteristics can help decisionmakers in choosing from a set of predefined alternative structures like those that we have presented. Such consideration can also inform planning and coordination among the myriad organizations preparing to respond to future disasters, providing a common ground for debate and decisionmaking in the event of a disaster. This would set the stage for a rapid decision regarding a $C^2$ structure (if such a quick decision is warranted and feasible) or, if appropriate, holding off on decisions regarding $C^2$ until the characteristics of the disaster have fully emerged. This approach could also provide for advance training of military forces under all of the $C^2$ alternatives. Units that are familiar with and have practiced under the chosen $C^2$ alternative would be able to fall into place quickly, perhaps eliminating some of the time required to gear up to a new and evolving $C^2$ structure.

Finally, it should be noted that there is no reason why the command relationships could not change during a disaster response. Indeed, using the criteria identified above, it is possible to envision a greater need for a federal lead during the early stages of a crisis, when state and local governments might have the most difficulty exercising $C^2$ because of their proximity to the disaster area. However, as the crisis begins to subside and the state regains its capacity to exercise control, command could be transferred back to state authorities. The critical point in this discussion is that $C^2$ issues need to be examined in advance to ensure that the alternative structures are understood by all parties.

# CHAPTER FIVE

# Conclusions

---

Hurricane Katrina, as catastrophic as it was, provides the United States with an opportunity to become better prepared for the future. The nation's response to this event was heroic, impressive, and unprecedented, but it was also tragically delayed in accomplishing rescues and evacuations and providing relief to affected citizens. The various lessons-learned reports chronicle the events of the storm and its aftermath, highlighting the many deficiencies of the response efforts. Numerous steps have been taken to improve the nation's readiness, including changes in the NRP and the ways that civilian and military operations are coordinated at all levels of government. While time will always be of the essence in catastrophic domestic emergencies, more can be done to prepare for a quicker and more robust response.

The lessons-learned reports provide a point of departure for this effort, but they, too, have limitations. They record the problems and potential remedies but fail to set priorities. No attempt is made to uncover where tensions and contradictions exist among the recommendations, and any estimate of the potential financial or other types of costs is rare. The lessons-learned reports also frequently cite deficiencies in areas that they do not define clearly, such as situational awareness. Our analysis indicates that decisionmakers in the days following Hurricane Katrina's landfall had considerable information about the dire straits of the citizens and the significant destruction to the infrastructure throughout Louisiana and Mississippi.

We documented how and why the major problems arose in the U.S. military's response to Hurricane Katrina to provide a basis for the design of future Army policies. In doing so, we gained an understanding of the constraints that will apply in any catastrophic emergency, but more important, we discovered that a future Army response will not look very different in the absence of changes to the ways in which the Army plans and operates in domestic emergencies. And, a future military response could be slower and smaller if a catastrophe occurs without warning, if there were to be multiple terrorist attacks across the United States and/or if more military forces are away overseas.

We uncovered courses of action that would make the military's ability to respond to domestic emergencies quicker and more robust, and we encourage their immediate adoption. One is for the DoD to give higher priority to developing its capability to respond to HLS emergencies by giving the National Guard the federal mission and funds to conduct HLS activities, as is the case in counterdrug operations. Another is for state governors and adjutants general to do more to prepare their National Guard units for quick deployments, not only within their states but for emergencies in other states. States need to develop plans for calling up units quickly, and governors must be prepared to call up their units on an involuntary basis to respond to emergencies out of state. States also need to make arrangements that provide coverage for National Guard units deployed overseas in the event of a domestic disaster. Transportation will be key to a quick response, and so ways need to be found to facilitate the movement of National Guard units across states via commercial or military aircraft.

A National Guard focus on preparations within and among states will not be sufficient. There needs to be a regional focus in the National Guard's preparations for catastrophic emergencies. This would encourage planning and exercising among various state National Guard units in a particular region, as well as with FEMA and other civilian organizations. To ensure that the National Guard response is quick and includes essential communications capabilities and personnel trained in HLS activities, we recommend the creation of ten regional task forces in the National Guard focused on preparing and responding quickly to HLS emergencies. Some of the force structure freed up by Army plans to reduce the number of National Guard combat brigades could be used to create regional Civil Support Battalions. These could be linked with National Guard division headquarters to enable their significant $C^2$ capabilities to move seamlessly into and out of an affected state whenever needed.

In a catastrophic emergency, National Guard and active-duty units need to arrive quickly; their response time can be improved through the Army's ARFORGEN process. While all Army units are available to respond to domestic emergencies, there is little being done to ready these forces specifically for HLS operations. This fact could be addressed through the implementation of specific HLS training and exercises for units in the Ready pool, in addition to their normal activities. Then, in assigning missions for units within the ARFORGEN process, some units could be given a specific HLS mission; these units would be linked regionally to the various civilian response agencies. These units could still be deployable overseas if needed, but they would be placed in the "theater-committed" ARFORGEN process category. The number and types of units given the HLS mission would be defined in light of currently available civilian responders; they could then be adjusted as civilian capabilities improve.

$C^2$ arrangements fit into a much broader system that involves the collection, processing, and delivery of the information that enables a commander to direct forces toward accomplishing a commonly understood goal and to maximize unity of effort. The $C^2$ structure is an important part of this system. But for a variety of reasons, it is not possible to decide on a single, predefined $C^2$ structure for all disaster response efforts, as the characteristics of domestic emergencies will differ in their requirements as will the capabilities of the states in which they may occur. Inevitably, there will also be tensions between state and federal officials over the control of forces. What can be done is to prepare officials to make the $C^2$ structure choices quickly by narrowing the range of potential alternatives and giving them an understanding of the disaster characteristics that would call for the adoption of a particular alternative. Continuing to leave this discussion until a disaster arises undermines the ability of responders to achieve unity of effort, given that the relief operations require support from so many different government organizations.

Some of these initiatives will cost money, but what is most needed is a change from past practices and in perspectives on the role and responsibility of the military in catastrophic domestic emergencies. Having military forces trained and ready for homeland security is no less important than for contingencies overseas.

# Situational Awareness in Hurricane Katrina

Information is critical to the ability of officials to design and implement the many different dimensions of a response to a domestic emergency. The various lessons-learned reports covering Hurricane Katrina often point to the lack of situational awareness among the leaders of the response efforts, though these report are often vague as to what they mean. The White House report states that the "lack of communications and situational awareness had a debilitating effect on the Federal response" and that the Secretary of Homeland Security "lacked real-time, accurate situational awareness."[1] The House report concluded that "among the most significant factors were a lack of communications and situational awareness."[2] According to the Senate report, situational awareness was deeply flawed.[3] This report particularly singled out the failure of officials located outside of New Orleans to quickly learn about the breach in the levees and the lack of information throughout the government about the thousands of people stranded in the convention center.[4]

Situational awareness can mean different things: information about conditions on the ground, a "common operating picture" of what is happening, knowledge of assets such as relief supplies. In our analysis, we chose to focus on the types of information that were avail-

---

[1]  The White House, *The Federal Response to Hurricane Katrina*, pp. 50, 52.

[2]  U.S. House, *A Failure of Initiative*, p. 188.

[3]  U.S. Senate, *Hurricane Katrina*, p. 9.

[4]  U.S. Senate, *Hurricane Katrina*, Chapter 19.

able to federal and state officials during the first week after Hurricane Katrina made landfall as they designed and implemented the overall civilian and military response.

What did decisionmakers know about the relief needs: the number of casualties, hospital patients, evacuees, and shelter victims and the availability of food and water? What information did they have about the damage to different types of infrastructure: communications and transportation networks, utilities, and hospitals? Was there information about the extent of the flooding, criminal activity, and public health in the disaster areas?

Our sources were the briefings and summaries that were generated daily in the DHS, JTF-Katrina, LOEP, and the Louisiana State Police. We reviewed information generated during the first week of the response, including the daily briefings from DHS and JTF-Katrina for August 30, August 31, September 2, and September 5. We also had information from LOEP and Louisiana State Police for three of these days: August 31, September 2, and September 5.

Table A.1 provides a general overview of what we found regarding the situational awareness of these organizations. A check mark a particular row in the figure indicates that the daily reports or briefings included information on the particular subject. The information was not always identical or equally detailed among the organizations. For example, with regard to the status of oil and gas utilities, on August 31, DHS reported information for each production site; JTF-Katrina reported similar information as well as notes on pipelines and production capability; and LOEP reported aggregate and detailed data for each parish.

What we discovered is that DHS, JTF-Katrina, and the Louisiana organizations had a good idea of what the situation looked like beginning soon after hurricane landfall in terms of relief needs, infrastructure damage, and criminal activity. From our research, it was not possible to ascertain the accuracy of the information or what information was shared; just that such information was available to support decisionmakers in the federal government and those in Louisiana in designing the response to Hurricane Katrina.

At the same time, there were a few important exceptions. While paying attention to the people and criminal activities in the Super-dome, these reports did not include information on the situation in the convention center until September 2, the day before the evacuations of that facility began. Only then did information regarding the conven-tion center appear in the DHS report that tracked the status of evacu-ations and in the Louisiana State Police report.[5] There is also very little information in the briefings and reports we reviewed as to the public health situation and almost no information on hospital patients and those in nursing homes.

We also reviewed daily reports or briefings from the NGB, NORTHCOM, the Chairman of the Joint Chiefs of Staff, the Assis-tant Secretary of Defense for Homeland Defense, and the Department of the Army. While these were not available for each of our sample days, we did find that they, too, had a good appreciation of the number of people in danger and the extent of the damage to the infrastructure, including the extent of the flooding in New Orleans. Their specific focus differed, however, with the NGB tracking the flow of National Guard personnel, the Department of the Army following the flow of all Army forces, and the Assistant Secretary for Homeland Defense describing the details of DoD mission assignments.

What we discovered in our analysis was that considerable infor-mation about the dire straits of people and the significant destruction to infrastructure was available to officials, enough for them to under-stand the capabilities required to ensure an effective response.

---

[5]   The situation report of the 5th Army on September 2, 2005, raised the need for the evac-uation of the convention center and estimated the number of people there to be 25,000.

**Table A.1**
**Strategic Situational Awareness**

| | DHS | | | | JTF-Katrina | | | | Louisiana Office of Emergency Preparedness | | |
|---|---|---|---|---|---|---|---|---|---|---|---|
| | Aug. 30 | Aug. 31 | Sept. 2 | Sept. 5 | Aug. 30 | Aug. 31 | Sept. 2 | Sept. 5 | Aug. 30 | Sept. 2 | Sept. 5 |
| **Relief needs** | | | | | | | | | | | |
| Casualties | | ✓ | ✓ | ✓ | ✓ | ✓ | ✓ | ✓ | ✓ | | |
| Hospital patients | | | ✓ | | | | | | | | |
| Evacuees | ✓ | ✓ | ✓ | ✓ | ✓ | ✓ | ✓ | ✓ | ✓ | ✓ | ✓ |
| Availability of food and water | | ✓ | ✓ | ✓ | ✓ | ✓ | ✓ | ✓ | ✓ | ✓ | ✓ |
| Number and location of shelter victims | ✓ | ✓ | ✓ | ✓ | ✓ | ✓ | ✓ | ✓ | ✓ | ✓ | ✓ |
| **Infrastructure damage** | | | | | | | | | | | |
| Telephone network availability, including cellular | ✓ | ✓ | ✓ | ✓ | ✓ | ✓ | ✓ | ✓ | ✓ | | ✓ |
| **Utilities** | | | | | | | | | | | |
| Water/wastewater system status | ✓ | ✓ | ✓ | ✓ | ✓ | ✓ | ✓ | ✓ | ✓ | ✓ | |
| Electricity/public lighting status | ✓ | ✓ | ✓ | | ✓ | ✓ | ✓ | ✓ | ✓ | ✓ | ✓ |

**Table A.1—Continued**

| | DHS | | | | JTF-Katrina | | | | Louisiana Office of Emergency Preparedness | | |
|---|---|---|---|---|---|---|---|---|---|---|---|
| | Aug. 30 | Aug. 31 | Sept. 2 | Sept. 5 | Aug. 30 | Aug. 31 | Sept. 2 | Sept. 5 | Aug. 30 | Sept. 2 | Sept. 5 |
| Oil and Gas status | ✓ | ✓ | ✓ | ✓ | ✓ | ✓ | ✓ | ✓ | ✓ | ✓ | ✓ |
| Transportation network | | | | | | | | | | | |
| Road closures (go/no-go terrain) | ✓ | | ✓ | ✓ | ✓ | ✓ | ✓ | ✓ | ✓ | ✓ | ✓ |
| Port status | ✓ | ✓ | ✓ | ✓ | ✓ | ✓ | ✓ | ✓ | ✓ | ✓ | ✓ |
| Condition of levees/drainage canals and extent of flooding | ✓ | ✓ | ✓ | ✓ | ✓ | ✓ | ✓ | ✓ | ✓ | ✓ | ✓ |
| Hospitals | ✓ | ✓ | ✓ | ✓ | ✓ | ✓ | ✓ | ✓ | ✓ | ✓ | ✓ |
| Criminal activity | | | | | | | | | | | |
| Crime trends/incidents | ✓ | ✓ | ✓ | ✓ | ✓ | ✓ | ✓ | ✓ | ✓ | ✓ | ✓ |
| Type of activity | | | ✓ | ✓ | ✓ | ✓ | ✓ | | ✓ | ✓ | ✓ |
| Location of activity | | | ✓ | | ✓ | ✓ | ✓ | | ✓ | ✓ | |

Table A.1—Continued

| | DHS | | | | JTF-Katrina | | | | Louisiana Office of Emergency Preparedness | | |
|---|---|---|---|---|---|---|---|---|---|---|---|
| | Aug. 30 | Aug. 31 | Sept. 2 | Sept. 5 | Aug. 30 | Aug. 31 | Sept. 2 | Sept. 5 | Aug. 30 | Sept. 2 | Sept. 5 |
| Public health | | | | | | | | | | | |
| Epidemiology | | | | √ | | √ | | | | | |
| Food monitoring and inspection | √ | | √ | √ | | √ | | | | | |
| Water quality | | | √ | √ | | √ | | | | | |
| HAZMAT situation | √ | √ | √ | √ | √ | | √ | √ | √ | √ | √ |

# References

Barbour, Haley, Governor of Mississippi, *Executive Order No. 939*, Jackson, Miss., August 26, 2005.

Blanco, Kathleen Babineaux, Governor of Louisiana, Letter to the President of the United States, August 27, 2005.

———, Letter to the President of the United States, August 28, 2005.

———, Letter to the President of the United States, September 2, 2005.

———, Draft Letter to the President of the United States, with attached Memorandum of Agreement, September 2, 2005.

———, Testimony before the Committee on Homeland Security and Governmental Affairs, U.S. Senate, February 2, 2006. As of February 5, 2007: http://hsgac.senate.gov/_files/020206Blanco.pdf

Blum, LTG H. Steven, Chief, National Guard Bureau, Statement Before Commission on National Guard and Reserves, May 3, 2006.

———, Testimony Before the Committee on Armed Services, Subcommittee on Terrorism, Unconventional Threats and Capabilities, House of Representatives, Second Session, 109th Congress, May 25, 2006.

Bradberry, Johnny B., "Written Testimony of Johnny B. Bradberry, Secretary, La. Department of Transportation and Development Secretary," *Challenges in a Catastrophe: Evacuating New Orleans in Advance of Hurricane Katrina*, U.S. Senate Committee on Homeland Security and Governmental Affairs, January 31, 2006. As of February 5, 2007: http://hsgac.senate.gov/index.cfm?Fuseaction=Hearings.Detail&HearingID=312

Chief of the National Guard Bureau, *Annual Review*, 1990.

Cecchine, Gary, Michael A. Wermuth, Roger C. Molander, K. Scott McMahon, Jesse Malkin, Jennifer Brower, John D. Woodward, Donna F. Barbisch, *Triage for Civil Support: Using Military Medical Assets to Respond to Terrorist Attacks*, Santa Monica, Calif.: RAND Corporation, MG-217-OSD, 2004. As of February 5, 2007: http://www.rand.org/pubs/monographs/MG217/index.html

CNN.com, "New Orleans Braces for Monster Hurricane," August 29, 2005. As of February 5, 2007:
http://www.cnn.com/2005/WEATHER/08/28/hurricane.katrina/

Davis, Lynn E., David E. Mosher, Richard R. Brennan, Michael D. Greenberg, K. Scott McMahon, Charles W. Yost, *Army Forces for Homeland Security*, Santa Monica: Calif.: RAND Corporation, MG-221-A, 2004.

Honoré, LTG Russel, Letter to Select Bipartisan Committee to Investigate the Preparation for and Response to Hurricane Katrina, February 21, 2006.

————, testimony before Committee on Homeland Security and Governmental Affairs, U.S. Senate, February 9, 2006.

Jarrell, Jerry D., Max Mayfield, Edward N. Rappaport, and Christopher W. Landsea, "The Deadliest, Costliest, and Most Intense United States Hurricanes From 1900 to 2000," National Oceanic and Atmospheric Administration Technical Memorandum NWS TPC-1, October 2001. As of February 5, 2007:
http://www.aoml.noaa.gov/hrd/Landsea/deadly/index.html

Joint Publication 1-02, *The Department of Defense Dictionary of Military and Associated Terms*, Washington, D.C.: Joint Staff, April 12, 2001, as ammended through March 22, 2007.

Joint Task Force Andrew (JTF Andrew), "Overview Brief," n.d.

Landreneau, MG Bennett C., Testimony Before Homeland Security and Governmental Affairs Committee, U.S. Senate, February 9, 2006.

Louisiana State Police, Emergency Operations Center, "Hurricane Katrina Situation Report," August 28, 2005, August 29, 2005, August 30, 2005, August 31, 2005.

Louisiana Office of Emergency Preparedness, "SITREP," August 27, 2005, August 28, 2005, August 29, 2005, August 31, 2005, September 1, 2005 September 2, 2005, September 3, 2005, September 4, 2005, September 5, 2005, September 6, 2005.

Louisiana Office of the Governor, *Proclamation No. 48 KBB 2005*, Baton Rouge, La., August 26, 2005

————, "Overview of Governor Kathleen Babineaux Blanco's Actions in Preparation for and Response to Hurricane Katrina," Response to U.S. Senate Committee on Homeland Security and Governmental Affairs Document and Information Request Dated October 7, 2005, and to the U.S. House of Representatives Select Committee to Investigate the Preparation for and Response to Hurricane Katrina, December 2, 2005. As of February 5, 2007:
http://www.gov.state.la.us/assets/docs/PDFs/Gov.response.12.2.05.pdf

McHale, Paul, Assistant Secretary of Defense for Homeland Defense, Testimony Before the Committee on Armed Services, Subcommittee on Terrorism,

Unconventional Threats and Capabilities, House of Representatives, May 25, 2006.

National Hurricane Center, Advisories, August 23, 2005–August 30, 2005.

———, "Hurricane Andrew, 1992," Web site, n.d. As of February 5, 2007:
http://www.nhc.noaa.gov/HAW2/english/history.shtml#andrew

National Guard Bureau, cable to state adjutants general, August 31, 2005.

———, *National Guard After Action Review: Hurricane Response September 2005*, December 21, 2005.

National Guard Bureau, GIS Staff, "Army National Guard Units in Support of Hurricane Disaster Area, Mississippi and Louisiana," September 9, 2005.

Office of Homeland Security, *National Strategy for Homeland Security*, July 2002. As of February 5, 2007:
http://www.whitehouse.gov/homeland/book/

Sprenger, Sebastian, *Inside the Pentagon*, August 31, 2006.

Tyson, Ann Scott, "Strain of Iraq War Means the Relief Burden Will Have to Be Shared," *Washington Post*, August, 31, 2005. As of February 5, 2007:
http://www.washingtonpost.com/wp-dyn/content/article/2005/08/30/AR2005083002162_pf.html

U.S. Air Force, "Civil Reserve Air Fleet," fact sheet, January 2007. As of February 5, 2007:
http://www.af.mil/factsheets/factsheet.asp?id=173

U.S. Army, Center for Army Lessons Learned, *Disaster Response Hurricanes Katrina and Rita Initial Impressions Report*, 2005.

———, "Special Defense Department Briefing with Commander of Joint Task Force Katrina," transcript, September 1, 2005. As of February 5, 20007:
http://www.defenselink.mil/transcripts/2005/tr20050901-3843.html

———, Institute of Land Warfare, "National Disaster Response: Hurricane Katrina," briefing, October 5, 2005.

———, *2006 Posture Statement*, February 10, 2006.

———, *Army Campaign Plan*, Annex F (ARFORGEN Implementation Plan) to Army Campaign Plan Change 4, July 27, 2006.

———, *Army Campaign Plan: National Guard*, briefing, n.d. As of February 5, 2007:
http://www.army.mil/thewayahead/acppresentations/3_2.html

U.S. Department of Defense, *Strategy for Homeland Defense and Civil Support*, Washington, D.C.: U.S. Department of Defense, June 2005. As of February 5, 2005:
http://www.defenselink.mil/news/Jun2005/d20050630homeland.pdf

U.S. Department of Defense, Office of the Assistant Secretary of Defense (Public Affairs), press briefings, August 31, 2005–September 9, 2005.

U.S. Department of Homeland Security, *National Incident Management System*, March 1, 2004. As of February 5, 2007:
http://www.fema.gov/pdf/emergency/nims/nims_doc_full.pdf

————, *National Response Plan*, December 2004.

————, "National Planning Scenarios," draft version 20.2, April 2005.

————, Situation Reports, August 29 through September 10, 2005.

————, "United States Government Response to the Aftermath of Hurricane Katrina," press release, August 31, 2005.

————, "Highlights of United States Government Response to the Aftermath of Hurricane Katrina," press release, September 10, 2005.

————, Office of the Inspector General, *A Performance Review of FEMA's Disaster Management Activities in Response to Hurricane Katrina*, March 2006.

————, *Notice of Change to the National Response Plan*, May 25, 2006.

————, Joint Letter to the President of the United States from Secretary Chertoff and Secretary Rumsfeld, April 7, 2006.

U.S. Armu, Headquarters Department of the Army Headquarters (G-3), "Katrina Update," briefing, September 1, 2005.

U.S. Government Accountability Office, *Homeland Defense: DOD Needs to Asses the Structure of U.S. Forces for Domestic Military Missions*, GAO-03-670, Washington, D.C: U.S. Government Accountability Office, July 2003.

U.S. Homeland Security Council, "Planning Scenarios: Executive Summaries," July 2004.

U.S. House of Representatives, *A Failure of Initiative*, Final Report of the Select Bipartisan Committee to Investigate the Preparation and Response to Hurricane Katrina, Washington, D.C.: U.S. Government Printing Office, February 2006.

U.S. Senate, *Hurricane Katrina: A Nation Still Unprepared*, Report of the Committee on Homeland Security and Governmental Affairs, Washington, D.C.: U.S. Senate, May 2006. Published in a slightly different form as Senate Special Report 109-322, as of February 5, 2007:
http://hsgac.senate.gov/_files/Katrina/FullReport.pdf

The White House, "President Addresses Nation: Discusses Hurricane Katrina Relief Efforts," Washington, D.C., September 3, 2005. As of February 5, 2007
http://www.whitehouse.gov/news/releases/2005/09/20050903.html

————, *The Federal Response to Hurricane Katrina: Lessons Learned*, February 2006. As of February 5, 2007:
http://www.whitehouse.gov/reports/katrina-lessons-learned.pdf

Warner, Senator John W., "Statement Made on the Senate Floor: DOD Hurricane Katrina Relief Efforts," September 15, 2005.

————, "Additional Views of Senator John Warner, Senate Committee on Homeland Security and Governmental Affairs, Hurricane Katrina Report," May 9, 2006. As of February 5, 2007:
http://hsgac.senate.gov/_files/Katrina/AVWarner.pdf

Wormuth, Christine E., Michele A. Flournoy, Patrick T. Henry, Clark A. Murdock, *The Future of the National Guard and Reserves*, Washington, D.C.: CSIS, July 2006.